The
Motorcycle
Book

First published in 2004 by Motorbooks International,
an imprint of MBI Publishing Company, Galtier Plaza,
Suite 200, 380 Jackson Street, St. Paul, MN
55101-3885 USA

Motorbooks International titles are also available at
discounts in bulk quantity for industrial or sales-
promotional use. For details write to Special Sales
Manager at Motorbooks International Wholesalers &
Distributors, Galtier Plaza, Suite 200, 380 Jackson
Street, St. Paul, MN 55101-3885 USA.

ISBN 0-7603-1745-3

Printed in the United Kingdom

The Motorcycle Book

Everything you need to know about owning, enjoying and maintaining your bike

Which motorcycle?
Training
Clothing
Insurance
Security
Luggage
Tires
Wheels
Brakes
Suspension
Frames
Engines
Tuning
Exhausts
Accessories
Electrics
Buying Used
Storage
Maintenance
Trouble-shooting

Alan Seeley

MOTORBOOKS
INTERNATIONAL

1
Which motorcycle?

2
Getting on the road

Know your motorcycle

Looking after your motorcycle

1

Which motorcycle?

Sportbikes represent the pinnacle of motorcycle evolution for fast road riding. Racing, they say, improves the breed, and the influence of competition development can be seen in the lines of many of today's superbikes.

Sportbikes

The manufacturers' relentless pursuit of more power from increasingly lighter and compact engines has put blistering performance in the hands of ordinary riders at affordable prices.

Two capacity groups dominate the sportbike sector: 600cc and the liter class. With about 100bhp on tap and top speeds in the 160mph bracket, it's easy to see the appeal of the 600s—especially if your age, experience, or driving record makes insurance premiums for larger capacity sportbikes prohibitively expensive. Fans of the class argue that there's no need for any more performance on the road, further justifying their stance by pointing to the lithe handling of these comparative lightweights.

Honda CBR900RR inline 4-cylinder 954cc, 130bhp, 370lb   *Aprilia RSVR 60° V-twin-cylinder 999cc, 113bhp, 363lb*

Suzuki GSX-R1000 inline 4-cylinder 988cc, 161bhp, 374lb

Some 600s are less compromising than others, making them ideal choices for riders who want to explore the outer limits of their bike's performance on the race track as well as on the road. Of the supersport 600s currently available, the Yamaha R6 and, to an only slightly lesser extent, the Suzuki GSX-R600 are the most single-minded. But their ultra-sharp handling and committed riding positions can be a bit much for riders who favor straight-line stability and comfort. Their first choices would be Kawasaki's incredibly capable ZX-6R, up to 636cc from 2002, or the bike that firmly established the class and dominated it for nearly a decade, Honda's venerable CBR600, now available in even sportier RR form with revised motor and chassis and optional race components.

An outside contender in the class is Triumph's TT600, a capable handler but lacking the power and refined delivery of its classmates.

If inline four-cylinder 600cc power isn't to your tastes, then Ducati's 748 provides a V-twin alternative with comparable power and peerless race-bred handling.

The liter division is seen by manufacturers and riders alike as the blue ribbon class of sportbikes. The benchmark was set by Honda's now-near-ubiquitous CBR900RR, and the 900 dominated the sector for most of the 1990s, eventually being

outperformed by Yamaha's R1, introduced in 1998. The current crop of 1000cc superbikes offers a winning combination of big-bore behemoth power from compact engines in sparse, nimble chassis. For 2001 Suzuki launched the GSX-R1000, a compelling package that sent bike designers from the other manufacturers scurrying back to their drawing boards. Meanwhile, Kawasaki's ZX-9R and Triumph's 955i founder in the competition's wake, worthy and capable though they are. If you want to go V-twin exotic, then look at Ducati's 996, Aprilia's RSV Mille or Honda's WSB-winning SP-1 and SP-2.

If cubes are your ultimate pursuit then consider Suzuki's Hayabusa, a 1300cc monster that can nudge 200mph yet still take you comfortably to work and even touring, or the Kawasaki ZX-12R. Both bikes were built to take the Honda Blackbird's fastest road bike crown, and despite their size they can be surprisingly nimble.

To fulfill a dream of a 750cc sportbike, there's only one real contender. Suzuki's GSX-R750 almost defies capacity classification and is a cult in its own right. If you fancy a stable and capable, if heavy, 750, then spring for the Kawasaki ZX-7R.

Whichever sportbike you opt for, don't worry if its performance is a little beyond you on road or track—you'll be able to make good use of your bike's figures in bar room bench racing.

Suzuki's GSX-R1000 topped the superbike list when it was launched for 2001, but who knows what Honda, Yamaha and Kawasaki have up their sleeves? Sportbikes are in a constant state of evolution.

They might sound a contradiction in terms, but today's sport tourers really do offer a decent all-around package. They're the first choice for the rider who demands comfort for serious mile-munching in a bike that can still cut it on a Sunday blast in the twisties.

Sport tourers

Kawasaki ZZ-R1200 inline four, 16-valve, 1164cc, 160bhp (claimed), 520lb (dry)

Honda VFR800 Fi V4 16-valve, 781cc, 104.6bhp (claimed), 462lb (dry)

Ducati ST4s V-twin, 8-valve, 996cc, 117bhp (claimed), 466lb (dry)

Sport touring bikes have really come into their own in recent years. Not so long ago, manufacturers used to apply the tag to sports models that had been superseded by their own latest, highly advanced offerings, rounding their harder edges and repackaging them as fast but friendly and comfortable all-rounders.

Today, manufacturers are wise to the needs of intrepid travelers who want the performance to take them where they want to go quickly, and the handling to let them exploit the most exciting route there. Of course there's nothing to stop you touring on a regular sportbike, but if you're planning to take a passenger, he or she is going to be pretty uncomfortable even before the first fuel stop, which will come around a lot quicker than on a sport tourer with its (usually) greater tank range.

The bike that defined the sport tourer class is Honda's VFR800, a V4 that now features the company's VTEC variable valve system to make the legendary motor even more flexible than its deserved reputation. Optional antilock braking makes for an even more refined package.

Where Honda led, others followed, even overtaking the VFR in some areas of performance. A good example is Triumph's Sprint ST, which features the 955cc motor from the sporty T595 Daytona retuned for more of the mid-range beloved of sport tourer pilots. Kawasaki set out a new marker in the class with its 2002 ZZ-R1200. With an engine based on that from the legendary ZZ-R1100 Rocketship, the new bike claims 160bhp at the crank to make it the most powerful bike in the sport tourer class. The ZZ-R12 also boasts levels of comfort on a par with some full-blown tourers.

By definition, any sport tourer is something of a compromise—there are better sportbikes and there are better tourers. But no sport tourer blurs the distinction between "sport" and "tourer" better than Ducati's ST4s. The Italian firm has taken the V-twin engine from the mighty 996, skimmed some power off the top, and fattened up the mid-range to create a bike that satisfies the sportiest of sport tourists. With its upside-down Showa forks and trademark Ducati trellis frame, the ST4s is basically a sportbike with a comfortable dual seat and a decent tank range.

If European twins are your thing, you might also like to look at Aprilia's Falco and Futura liter V-twins and BMW's R1100S shaft-drive boxer.

Because their performance is a little down on their full-on sports brethren's and insurers perceive them as tending to attract more "sensible" riders, sport tourers fall into similar insurance groups as 600cc sportbikes, although they frequently cost a bit more to buy. But if you compare the price of buying close to big-bore sportbike performance against lower premiums, sport tourers start to look like very good values indeed.

Tourers

In theory you can tour on any bike you like, just as, in theory, you can cross the Atlantic in a canoe. But if your aspirations are more first class than leaky raft, you'll want a full-blown tourer for your high-mileage excursions.

BMW K1200LT inline 4-cylinder 16-valve, 1171cc. 98bhp (claimed), 831lb (dry)

Honda's Gold Wing represents the pinnacle of grand touring. In its current incarnation, the Wing boasts a huge 1832cc, flat six-cylinder, fuel-injected motor, pumping out a claimed 123ft-lb of torque at a lowly 4000rpm—more than enough to push along its 799lb. A massive 6.5-gallon fuel tank allows you to cover the length of small countries between fuel stops. Just activate the cruise control, sit back, and enjoy the ride. An optional six-CD auto-changer provides the entertainment on the more boring stretches, or you can talk to your passenger in their armchair-like seat over the intercom. Feeling the windblast? Simply adjust the screen or combat the chill by opening the heater vents, which divert warm air from the engine toward the rider.

There's plenty of room in the lockable panniers—nearly 150 liters – to stash snacks and souvenirs.

The Wing's bulk makes it difficult to carve through traffic like you can on other bikes, but it's otherwise surprisingly nimble for its size. There's even a reverse gear, should you find the need.

Looking at the Wing now, it's hard to believe that it was originally conceived as a sportbike. But that was back in the 1970s, when bigger-bore motors were seen as the only way to go for performance. Honda soon wised up and the Wing went down another evolutionary path.

If the Wing's opulence seems a little over the top, then smaller tourers are available, but some are almost as well appointed, such as BMW's K1200LT.

Sportbike purists may scoff at the big touring bikes, arguing that they have all the disadvantages of a car with none of the advantages of a bike. But with excellent weather protection and superior comfort, maybe the tourers are having the last laugh. In any case, they can't hear you above their CD players.

Taking a peek under the skin of Honda's mighty GL1800 Gold Wing. Big everything. Luxurious seating (bottom left), note speakers and intercom jack. "What does this button do, Dad?" (center). Holds everything but the kitchen sink (bottom right). Be sure to check for stowaways.

Standards occupy motorcycling's middle ground, for price and performance—and not forgetting insurance classification.

Standards

Ducati Monster 750 air-cooled V-twin, 4-valve, 748cc, 66bhp (claimed), 403lb (dry)

Suzuki GSF600 Bandit inline 4-cylinder 16-valve, 599cc, 78.9bhp (claimed), 431lb (dry)

Bikes such as the BMW F650, Honda Nighthawk 650, and Suzuki Bandit 600 are ideal first choices for riders who have recently passed their tests. Their user-friendly riding positions and power delivery make for a package that won't intimidate less experienced riders, or rush them headlong into trouble.

Bikes in this class make great all-rounders, even if they don't excel at anything in particular—apart from providing relatively cheap fun.

They lack sportbike levels of ground clearance, so crazy lean angles are out. But there's enough there for you to cut your trackday teeth on, should you choose. Bikes such as the FZ6 and 919 Interceptor have detuned engines from earlier Yamaha and Honda sportbikes. They might lack the top end of the original sportbike incarnations, but the engines have plenty of mid-range for punchy acceleration. Wind and weather protection is minimal on standards since they are usually unfaired—although some have windscreens or half fairings—so they wouldn't be first choice for touring.

Standards are built using conventional components, and this is reflected in their cost. Frames are usually cheap tubular steel, not the aluminum alloy spars of sportbikes. Suspension is usually functional, but low-buck and non-adjustable. But, pound for pound, standards represent great fun.

At the less sparkling end of the performance spectrum lie bikes such as the Buell Blast and Suzuki GS500E. Honda's Nighthawk and Kawasaki's ZR-7 still provide an option in the 750 four-cylinder standard class. The FZ6 and 919 offer performance close to sportbikes. If you want something different, go for the Italian Cagiva Raptor 650 or the Suzuki SV650, both of which use a 645cc V-twin engine from the Japanese company. And there are Ducati's 620 and 750cc air-cooled V-twin Monsters.

So even if a standard can't give you a total sportbike buzz, the money you'll save on insurance, servicing, and fuel provides plenty of compensation.

Suzuki SV650 liquid-cooled V-twin-cylinder 8-valve, 645cc, 70bhp (claimed), 363lb (dry)

Kawasaki ER-5 parallel twin-cylinder 8-valve, 498cc, 50bhp (claimed), 383lb (dry)

Suzuki GS500E parallel twin, 487cc, 51.3bhp (claimed), 381lb (dry)

Retros

One of the broadest categories of motorcycles. Retros cover everything from bikes that look like 1960s throwbacks with roughly similar performance to the machines that give them their styling cues, to big-bore unfaired muscle bikes that don't really deserve the tag at all.

Kawasaki's W650 and Triumph's Bonneville twins faithfully evoke the spirit of a bygone age. For riders who fancy the look, but not the intensive maintenance, of an older bike, they're ideal choices, although you'll need to keep the polishing rag handy for all that chrome. They're not huge on horses—the W650 claims slightly less than 50bhp while the 790cc Triumph claims just over 60. The real back wheel figures will be close to those of the 1960s bikes they mimic. Overhead camshafts and electric starters will be unfamiliar to those who remember pushrod engines and kick-starts, twin-shock rear suspension lives on in a world where the monoshock is the standard. Same goes for the air rather than liquid cooling of the engines. And, of course, owners of these modern classics can enjoy the image with the reassurance that their bikes have 21st century brakes and reliability.

At the other end of the scale sit big-bore musclebikes such as Yamaha's V-Max and Kawasaki's ZRX, whose commanding presence makes them look meaner than they really are.

Another Suzuki, the 1200 Bandit, is a cult in its own right, with a motor derived from the company's legendary, bulletproof GSX-R1100. For many years the Bandit 12 was the naked hooligan weapon of choice, but now it has some serious competition.

Yamaha's FZ-1 has a retuned motor from the R1 sportbike—less top end but loads in the middle. And where it beats its contemporaries, apart from performance, is in its handling. Where other bikes in the class tend to offer big motors in budget chassis, the Yam skimps in neither department—but that is reflected in the list price.

Honda followed the big Yamaha into the fray with the 919. Its chassis is less well appointed than the Yam's, but it is cheaper and uses an engine from an earlier CBR900RR, again retuned to take some off the top and boost the middle.

If you want a V-twin in the big naked class, look at Cagiva's Suzuki TL1000-engined Raptors. Ducati's 900 Monsters are popular too.

Retros, musclebikes—call them what you will—are huge fun. They're cheaper to insure than the latest cutting-edge sportbikes but give you at least as much to grin about.

Suzuki Bandit 1200 inline 4-cylinder 16-valve, 1157cc, 110bhp (claimed), 485lb (dry)

Yamaha FZ-1 inline 4-cylinder 20-valve, 998cc, 141bhp (claimed), 458lb (dry)

Kawasaki W650 parallel twin-cylinder 8-valve, 676cc, 49.6bhp (claimed), 429lb (dry)

Kawasaki ZRX1200R inline 4-cylinder 16-valve, 1164cc, 120bhp (claimed), 491lb (dry)

Cruisers

For more show than go, a cruiser is the perfect bike choice. The classic cruiser configuration is a V-twin motor slung in a long, low frame with a huge wheelbase and low-slung footpegs that mean aggressive cornering is firmly off the agenda. Those low footpegs combine with low, comfortable seats and wide bars to give a lazy riding position ideal for cruising at modest speeds.

Harley-Davidson VRSCA V-Rod V-twin 8-valve, 1130cc, 115bhp (claimed), 614lb (dry)

Suzuki VL1500LC Intruder V-twin 6-valve, 1462cc, 66bhp (claimed), 642lb (dry)

Suzuki GZ250 single 4-valve, 249cc,
20bhp (claimed), 302lb (dry)

Kawasaki VN1500 Mean Streak V-twin 8-valve,
1470cc, 72bhp (claimed), 669lb (dry)

*Love 'em or loathe 'em,
there is no class of bike
more likely to provoke
extreme devotion or extreme
derision than cruisers. So
just sit back and enjoy the
scenery and the easy riding
of motorcycling's showiest
showboats.*

Harley-Davidsons epitomize the cruiser style, and for many purists anything else is a feeble imitation. But these days most manufacturers offer a cruiser based on the famous Harley lines. Most feature V-twin motors in a lowly state of tune, designed to deliver optimum torque from minimal revs. They come in all sizes, from Honda's 250cc Rebel and Yamaha's Virago 250 to big-bore monsters like that same company's 1600cc Road Star. Despite its massive displacement, the Road Star manages to pump out only 58bhp at an "is-it-running?" 4200rpm, while making a massive 91ft-lb of torque at 2250rpm. See what we mean about massive torque and low power?

One exception to the V-twin cruiser rule is Honda's Valkyrie, which has an outrageous 1520cc flat six-cylinder motor that used to live in the Gold Wing. Again, torque is the thing, with a claimed 95.9ft-lb.

Moto Guzzi has various V-twin cruiser alternatives, but this time the cylinders are arranged across the frame rather than in line with it.

Most cruisers boast enough chrome to keep even the most avid of polishers happy, and if your

bike of choice doesn't have quite enough shiny bits for you, there is an endless array of aftermarket bolt-ons to let you customize your steed. If that still doesn't make it sufficiently eye-catching, you can always fit some slash-cut monster pipes to herald your arrival.

You get plenty of metal for your money with cruisers, and most are as heavy as their performance is ponderous.

Harley lookalikes became popular because they were often more refined than the Milwaukee vibrators from which they unashamedly stole their looks. Liquid-cooled engines, overhead camshafts, and shaft drive were niceties not to be found on the more traditional Harleys, whose harder edges play a big part in their appeal to devotees. But maybe things have come full circle with the Harley V-Rod, a liquid-cooled, double overhead cam, eight-valve V-twin that can haul its 614-pound self up the standing quarter mile in 11.5 seconds. Purists will be pleased to hear that the long wheelbase, low seat, wide bars, and forward pegs are still present and correct. But what to call the thing? A sport cruiser?

Dual sports are the 4x4s of the
motorcycling world—go-anywhere
machines that open up whole new
biking vistas. Most dualies make
reasonably usable road bikes, with
dual-purpose tires available to
replace dirt knobbies, but some
have more off-road purpose
than others.

Dual sports

Suzuki DRZ400 single-cylinder 4-valve, 398cc, 39bhp (claimed), 290lb (dry)

Trail riders largely prefer the light weight and simplicity of a two-stroke—Kawasaki's KMX125 and KDX series spring to mind in this category. Four-strokes are heavier but tend to offer more longevity than a stroker—Honda's XLR125 and Suzuki's DR125 are top choices here.

Going up a bit in capacity, Suzuki's DR-Z400S four-stroke has proved popular since its introduction in 2000. It replaced the DR350, a favorite of clubman enduro event off-road riders, and packs a torquey 398cc motor in a compact, motocross-style chassis. An ideal choice for the trails.

Specialist manufacturers such as Beta, Husqvarna, and KTM bring years of off-road market experience to bear on their dirt bikes.

Beta has only a small distribution in this country, but its Alp 125 and 200 are four-stroke bikes that

draw on its trials heritage while offering more general purpose.

The Husqvarna WRE125 is a gorgeous little two-stroke that also happens to a good starter bike. And the company's TE610E is a big four-stroke thumper for dedicated trail riders.

KTM has an excellent choice of off-roaders for the trail rider, from 250cc two-strokes to 625cc four-strokes, but they're more for the dirt than the tarmac.

Trail riding is an excellent way to discover old byways that have escaped the scourge of civilization, but bicycle and footpaths are off limits. If you have to use the street to get to the good stuff, your bike must be road-legal. Stay on the trail, be courteous to other users and respect the environment. That way, trail riding will continue to be one of the great outdoor pursuits.

Honda's XR650 (facing page) gives plenty of four-stroke grunt and torque without imposing too big a weight penalty on the trail rider. Looks like this guy's having fun, and that's what trail riding's all about. It's as dirty as you can get with your clothes on.

Kawasaki KDX125 single-cylinder 2-stroke, 124cc, 12/24bhp (claimed, restricted/derestricted), 235lb (dry)

Honda XLR125R single-cylinder 2-valve, 124.1cc, 11.4bhp (claimed), 262lb (dry)

Honda XL650V Transalp V-twin 6-valve, 647cc, 54.3bhp (claimed), 420lb (dry)

Adventure Tourers

They might take their styling cues from off-roaders, but adventure tourers aren't really for the rough stuff unless you have the strength and abilities of a Paris-Dakar desert racing hero.

BMW R1150GS flat twin 8-valve, 1130cc, 85bhp (claimed), 482lb (dry)

Suzuki V-Strom V-twin 8-valve, 996cc, 98bhp (claimed), 464lb (dry)

Aprilia Capo Nord V-twin 8-valve, 997.6cc, 98bhp (claimed), 473lb (dry)

Adventure tourers are imposing machines. You can make an aggressive Paris–Dakar statement on the road, even if your off-road ambitions extend no further than bumping on to the pavement outside the coffee shop.

Despite their looks, adventure tourers excel best on the road, especially in town. High riding position and wide bars make for a great view of the road and easy steering. Big-bore engines display a huge appetite for gobbling up miles. And huge fuel tanks extend the range between gas stations. But while the soft suspension delivers a comfortable ride, it also means cornering potential isn't in the sportbike league, and that upright riding position puts you right in the windblast. Still, if sportbikes aren't your bag, a big dual sport might be the thing.

Aprilia's Capo Nord is a good example of an adventure tourer. With a 997cc V-twin engine taken from Aprilia's sportier big twins (detuned to make less than 100bhp), the Capo Nord is a big softie that also has a harder edge when you turn it up a bit. A tall screen takes away the worst of the wind.

Cagiva's Navigator offers a similar package, its V-twin engine taken from Suzuki's TL1000.

BMW's flat twin R1150GS is the largest and latest of two decades' worth of big Beemer dual-sports. GS stands for "Gelande/Strasse," which translates roughly into English as "off-road/road," so you can see where the regular Paris to Dakar winning firm is coming from.

Other options include Kawasaki's well-loved KLR650. Triumph's 955cc Tiger triple is popular too, as is Yamaha's TDM twin, which was taken from 850cc to 900cc for 2002.

If the trail bike style is your thing but you need less than a liter in the engine department, look at bikes such as the Honda XR650, a four-stroke single, which is ideal for newer riders or commuters, or the BMW F650GS single—a 50bhp four-stroke. Suzuki's V-Strom 600 and 1000cc offerings make good V-twin alternatives.

Adventure tourers or "big trailies" are extremely popular in continental Europe, and make sound sense as capable all-rounders. Best to stick to the pavement, though.

Supermotos

Supermotos are the new kids on the biking block and have enjoyed a huge upsurge in interest over the past decade. Supermoto racing is huge in Europe, but has recently returned to the US and is fast gaining a foothold in the United Kingdom.

KTM Duke single-cylinder, 4-valve, 625cc. 55bhp (claimed), 319lb (dry)

CCM 604e Supermoto single-cylinder, 598cc air-cooled, 53bhp (claimed), 304lb (dry).

When you buy most supermotos, you essentially get a race bike with the legal niceties of lights, indicators, and a speedo tacked on. Usually big four-stroke singles, supermotos are being marketed to road riders as fun alternatives to sportbikes for those riders who don't trust themselves to stick to license-conserving speeds. And there's something in that. Big, torquey motors and low gearing make them a blast off the line, and if wheelies light your fire, a supermoto will more than happily oblige. Dynamite brakes and light weight make stoppies a breeze too. And top speeds rarely exceed 100mph, keeping licenses safe. On the other hand, high riding positions and big, thumping single cylinders aren't much fun on long straights, and small fuel tanks limit mileage between refills.

However, invest in a spare set of wheels for off-road tires and you have two bikes for the price of one (plus a set of wheels, of course). Most supermotos come with trick, high-quality, off-road suspension, which is more than adequate on road.

European companies dominate the supermoto market. British firm CCM has recently switched from Rotax power to Suzuki single engines. It builds stripped-down competition-derived machines, as well as slightly more refined offerings with larger fuel tanks for more road-going versatility.

Austrian firm KTM is another big name in supermotos, thanks to plenty of competition success. The KTM 640 Duke is a 625cc four-stroke single and production is limited to 1,500 bikes per year. There's also the LC4 Supermoto, which boasts the same engine but more basic off-road styling.

Italian firm Husqvarna (formed originally in Sweden) has the 449cc four-stroke SM450R, the supermoto version of its TE450 enduro bike. Husky also offers the TE610e—a dual sport, but even taller than the 450, which like all supermotos has a very high seat.

Supermotos are plenty of fun. Putting a big off-roader on 17-inch road wheels with sticky rubber is a surefire recipe for loads of laughs. Just stay away from the straights.

Supermoto racing is enjoying a renaissance in the 21st century. Major cities in the US and UK are reverberating to the sound of supermotos, as they thunder and backslide through improvised and purpose-built circuits for major televised race events. All competitiveness aside, supermotos are sure to find a foothold in the inner cities as corner-carving commuters look for something with more presence and punch than a scooter to haul them to work and back.

Supermotos started as a cult that is now gaining huge momentum. Mainly the pressure of specialist manufacturers, it won't take long for the large bike companies to move in on the action.

Commuters

Any motorcycle can be used as a commuter bike, but some are more suited than others. Riding a sportbike, say, through the cut and thrust of an urban rush hour can be a royal pain in the neck and wrists, apart from the fact that those bikes are geared for far longer-legged riding. A scooter is a great choice provided your ride to work is over mainly low-speed roads. But lightweights and middleweights are the best overall.

Yamaha FZ6 inline 4-cylinder 16-valve, 600cc, 98bhp (claimed), 423lb (dry)

Two simple reasons make an unfaired lightweight or middleweight—rather than a scooter—the top choice of commuter bike. First, they're less likely to attract the attention of thieves when parked outside work all day. Second, if you do have an unplanned get off in the free-for-all that is modern city riding, the bike is likely to sustain minimal damage. Even the lightest tumble on a faired sportbike is likely to result in a hefty bill because of the costly panels that make up the fairing.

The best alternatives to the city bus or the train are capable middleweights such as the Yamaha FZ6 and Honda Nighthawk. The new Suzuki GS500F and Kawasaki Ninja 500s make good choices too, although they're a little more conspicuous than their blander brethren.

The Honda Nighthawk 750 is a commuter staple that seems to have been around forever. This in-line four bike comes with hydraulically-adjusting valves (hence low maintenance) and derives from the CB750 that rocked the motorcycle world in the 1970s (the Nighthawk 750 first appeared in the early 80s and has barely changed since). So there's a recommendation of everyday reliability.

The bottom line is that there are plenty of bikes capable of playing the commuter role, offering an undemanding ride and low maintenance. Just as important, they provide an economic alternative to other means of commuting. And that has to be reason enough to rip up your bus pass and extend your motorcycling enjoyment to the everyday task of getting to work and back.

Look at this. BMW's F650 uses a dummy tank to make it the largest capacity, ride-to-work handbag on the planet. Add to that a belt final drive and it has to be a top choice for commuters who prefer to keep bike maintenance to a minimum.

Suzuki GS500E parallel twin, 487cc, 51.3bhp (claimed), 381lb (dry)

Honda Nighthawk 250 vertical twin 2-valve, 487cc, 20.1bhp (claimed), 287lb (dry)

Starter bikes

Rider training programs generally use bikes 250cc or less, and with good reason. A smaller starter bike affords you all the fun of riding on two wheels in a package that is easier to handle, lighter, smaller, and less expensive.

Kawasaki Eliminator 125 single-cylinder 2-valve, 124cc, 12bhp (claimed), 290lb (dry)

Honda CG125 single-cylinder 4-valve, 124cc, 10.8bhp (claimed), 301lb (dry)

The eighth- and quarter-liter bikes from Japan are established as training school staples, and it's easy to see why. The bulletproof little singles and twins can take as much punishment as even the most novice learner can throw at it, and being smaller they're economical too. Sure, they aren't exactly the most attractive bikes on the planet, but they're more than capable enough for learning on and make a useful commuter bike once you've passed your test. Starters' brakes are somewhat primitive and engines do not offer much freeway power, but it's enough to get you there.

You can, of course, learn to ride on a starter bike, but if you want your own and the simplicity of a 125 lacks the tough image you desire, there are loads of other small bikes that mimic the various bigger bikes. Honda offers a Rebel 250; the sporty CB250 Nighthawk; the XR100 or 250 dirt bikes (light kits can make them adaptable to street use); and the awesome new Magna 250.

Yamaha has the XT225 dual sport, the funky TW200, and the Rebel 250's main competition, the V-twin Virago 250.

Suzuki options extend to the four-stroke DR200SE dual sport and the GZ250 beginning cruiser.

Kawasaki provides the muscular-looking125 Eliminator and the taller but nimble and entertaining KL250 Super Sherpa.

Off-road specialist Husqvarna offers a interesting starter bike—knobbie-tired WRE125, but peaky power delivery and uncompromising off-road competition suspension make them perhaps not the best choice for novices interested in learning.

Dreaming of a 125cc sportbike? Aprilia's RS50 is a gorgeous two-stroke racer replica that looks and performs the part. The Buell Blast is a little larger at 492cc, but its light weight and low seat height make it easy to ride, with a belt final drive and self-adjusting valves keep it low maintenance.

There's plenty of choice in the small bike market and, just as important, something to suit most budgets.

Suzuki GZ125 single-cylinder, 2-valve, 124cc, 12bhp (claimed), 275lb (dry)

Reflect your post-test bike aspirations in your choice of 125 for your learner days. Sport, custom, cruiser, trailies, or standard— they're all there in the eighth-of-a-liter class.

Kawasaki KLR250 single-cylinder, 4-valve, 249cc, 258lb (dry)

Yamaha SR125 single-cylinder 2-valve, 124cc, 12bhp (claimed), 229lb (dry)

Classic bikes

If the latest tackle doesn't light your wick, what about a classic? People are drawn to classics for different reasons. Some older riders choose the bikes they either owned in their youth or couldn't afford back then. Other people just want to own and ride a legendary make or model. The simple satisfaction of keeping an old machine on the road can be a draw, too. And then there are the restorers, who buy machines to return them to original factory condition—known as "concours"—to show or to ride.

Given that bikes have been around for more than a century, there's plenty of choice. A pre-WW II single with a leather drive belt and only one gear might not make the best choice for a ride-to-work bike in the 21st century. So if you plan to use your classic bike fairly frequently, go for something more recent—especially if you're looking at your first classic. It will be easier to find parts, particularly if your classic was a popular model because many entrepreneurs are remanufacturing sought-after parts, often improving on the original components.

By going for a classic, you're turning your back on at least two decades of machine development. For regular use, choose a classic with enough performance to keep pace with modern traffic, and remember that braking and reliability will not be as good as with modern machinery. Even so, there are a number of specialists supplying conversions to upgrade brakes, replace points with electronic ignition, and generally make classics perform better and more reliably.

A huge network of classic enthusiast and owner clubs exists to help keep older machinery on the road, so join a club relevant to your bike. Clubs are an indispensable source of advice and many have great networks for spare parts, even going as far as remanufacturing parts if enough owners commit to buying them. They also organize runs and rallies, and many have regular local meetings, which are excellent opportunities to socialize with like-minded enthusiasts.

For many classic fans, the challenge of keeping their bikes on the road and the extra maintenance they tend to demand is all part of the fun—and most older bikes are far easier to work on than modern bikes, which is probably just as well.

As an added incentive, insurance for classics (because they're uncommon and crashed less often) is usually cheap, but it pays to shop around a little. And bikes 20 years or older (varies by state) qualify for special plates and exemptions, though also certain restrictions. So you'll have a bit more cash for spare parts and gasoline.

There are endless classics to choose from, but ideal selections for those new to the joys of older machines of character are the more common recent bikes for ease of parts availability and, in the case of bigger bikes, usable performance.

1973 Norton 850 Commando
parallel twin OHV, 748cc, 396lb (dry approx)

1981 Laverda Formula Mirage
inline triple DOHC, 1116cc, 510lb (dry)

Late Sixties Triumph Bonneville
parallel twin OHV, 649cc, 385lb (dry approx)

Scooters

The scooter market has been motorcycling's biggest boom area in the past few years, but it's more than a passing fad. Scooters offer a cheap and convenient alternative to a car—or even a bus pass. Fashion has played its part in the scooter's rise, but low running costs and cheap insurance are the real clinchers. Small, light, and easy to park, scooters are the ultimate solution for battling through the urban jungle. Add in fuel consumption that redefines 'frugal'—65mph is the average, and some will happily do close to 100mph—and scooters are a compelling option.

Aprilia Scarabeo
single-cylinder two stroke,
100/125cc, 92/140kg (dry)

Scooters are a tempting option for many reasons, including their ease of riding. Many are fully automatic—just twist the throttle and go. Most have enough storage space under the seat to store your helmet when you park, and accommodate a generous load of groceries for the ride home.

It's fitting that scooters are again finding their place transporting urban commuters and riders, because that's how they originally came into being. After the Second World War, there was a huge need for cheap transportation in Italy. Airplane factories were banned from making planes, but they still had the steel-pressing machinery and a surplus of small wheels from making fighters. Out of this adversity, the original Vespa ("wasp") was born, and Italy got on the road again.

Many of today's most desirable scooters are Italian—Piaggio, Vespa, Aprilia. The French are big players too, in the form of Peugeot. And, of course, the Japanese manufacturers would never miss a market. So there's plenty of choice in this very competitive arena.

Suzuki, Yamaha, and Honda have been particularly active in creating a new class of superscooter and the Italians are getting in on the act too. These machines combine scooter levels of comfort and weather protection with top speeds (about 100mph) that allow them to keep up with freeway traffic.

But are these scooters or are they bikes? Honda has its 582cc SilverWing, Piaggio the X9 500, Suzuki the Burgman 400 and Yamaha the 500 TMax. There comes a point when the nimble attributes of the smaller scooters are compromised by the manufacturers' desire to be all things to all people.

Italjet Dragster single-cylinder two-stroke, 50/125/180cc, 187/235/240 (dry)

Honda @125 single-cylinder four-stroke, 13bhp (claimed), 264lb (dry)

Suzuki Burgman single-cylinder 4-valve, 385cc, 32bhp (claimed), 383lb (dry)

Italjet Torpedo (above)
Scooter manufacturers are more than happy to tilt their hats to their heritage with swoopy lines and classic styling, while incorporating modern niceties such as disc brakes and indicator lights.

Mopeds

Not so long ago it was every 16-year-old's dream to own a moped, and the little fifties introduced many riders to a lifetime of motorcycling. Now the scooter boom has revived interest in motorcycling's mini marvels.

Light weight and ease of operation characterize mopeds. If you're younger than 16, they're generally your only powered two-wheeled option. Fortunately, there are numerous options from which to choose.

Aprilia SR50 Di Tech Racing
single-cylinder two-stroke, 50cc, 196lb (dry)

A moped is still the only way for anyone under 16 to use a powered machine on the road legally, and opens up a whole new world of freedom. Okay, there are limits. Top speed is 30mph, maximum power is usually 2bhp, and maximum engine size is 50cc. Options are somewhat limited because US consumers value larger size and horsepower than mopeds are allowed. But while mopeds might not be big on speed and power, they don't have to be small on style.

There are plenty of mopeds to choose from, though you may have to cross the Atlantic for the right one. Top scooter-style options include Aprilia's SR50LC sports moped and the Rally LC trail-style scooter moped. If you prefer trail-style mopeds pick from the Aprilia RX50, Derbi Senda R, Gilera H@K, and Suzuki TS50X, among others.

Scooters are huge in Italy and other Italian companies such as Benelli, Beta, Gilera, Italjet, Malaguti, MBK, Piaggio, and, of course, Vespa have some stylish scooter-mopeds too—as does Spanish firm Derbi. France isn't known as a big producer of bikes, but Peugeot's 50cc Speedfight has been a huge sales success largely because of its styling and handling.

The Japanese ignore few markets, and mopeds are no exception. Honda, Suzuki, and Yamaha all offer scooter-style fifties. If you're limited to moped performance but demand envious looks, consider Yamaha Zuma, the Honda Metropolitan II, or the more powerful Suzuki AY50 K3—and head straight to the top of the school bikerack style charts.

Mopeds are fun and economical, if lacking in power. A lot of mopeds are restricted, so the potential for more power is there. However, this can put the bike outside the scope of your license—assuming the powers that be find out—and affect warranties and insurance coverage. Either way, they're a great introduction to the joys of motorcycling.

Yamaha Zuma single-cylinder two-stroke, 49cc, 185lb (dry)

Honda SH50 City Express single-cylinder two-stroke, 49cc, 3.8bhp (claimed), 150lb (dry)

2

Getting
on the road

Starting
out

Having decided you want to go motorcycling, you need to prepare yourself for the road ahead. While a motorcycle license is required, and there are numerous ways of getting the endorsement you need to ride. Other considerations such as training, riding gear, the size and type of bike you select, and insurance should factor into your decisions, as well.

Cut your riding teeth on a blue funky moped (left) . . . then move up to the giddy power of a CG125 (right)

A nearly infinite number of ways exist to go from complete rookie to licensed rider. But the stages involved are very similar from state to state. Some of the steps are legal requirements and others are matters of personal choice. Having all of your i's dotted and your t's crossed will mean you are ready to hit the streets as a properly-endorsed motorcycle rider.

Mopeds are a great option for a first bike because they are fun to ride and a low-cost way to learn the ropes of motorcycling. Awesome fuel economy and automatic transmissions make for great starter bikes. In many states, any licensed driver can operate a moped on the street. In some states, a resident without a driver license can ride a moped on the street with only a moped permit. This makes a very attractive choice for those below legal driving age or anyone who wants to gradually ease into their personal two-wheeled journey.

Nearly every state has a learner permit system in place for new motorcycle riders. A permit is a temporary license that allows you to practice and ride on the street to prepare for your skill test. The permit is usually attainable with a knowledge and vision test, though some jurisdictions require you to demonstrate your skills, as well. Most motorcycle permits are subject to restrictions such as daytime only, no passengers, cycle size restrictions, helmet use, etc.

Training is generally not required, but is highly encouraged by most state licensing agencies. Nearly every state offers some type of public or private training. About one third of states require minors or riders under 21 to complete an approved training course to earn their motorcycle endorsement. Most states will waive some or all of the required tests for the motorcycle license for an adult rider who completes a course. Research shows that rider training is a particularly effective countermeasure to crashing for the first six months after the training. States know this and try to help make a training course worth your time.

Besides helping to sidestep some or all of the licensing process, a safety course also offers other benefits. Classroom discussion focuses on the mental aspects of riding such as preparation, attitude, riding strategy, and alcohol. The riding portion of the course uses supervised practice on a closed course in critical motorcycle handling skills. Some insurance companies and other businesses offer discounts to course graduates, as well.

After you navigate the hills and curves of the learner permit process and motorcycle training, it is time to go get your motorcycle endorsement. To ride unrestricted on public roadways, every motorcyclist needs a license. The state in which you live will measure your skill and knowledge as a motorcyclist and then award you with the magic "M" on your driver license. You will probably be required to pay a modest fee for the privilege.

Remember, though, getting the license does not mean you are an expert rider, or even that you are a safe rider. Learning to ride a motorcycle is like learning to play the piano—after twenty or so hours of practice, you may feel as if you have accomplished a lot in a very short time, but you have much more to learn. And the only way to do it is through practice. Just because you passed the test, can shift through the gears, and can start on a hill does not mean you're ready for everything that comes your way. Be aware of your limitations, ride accordingly, and practice.

After taking training and receiving a motorcycle endorsement, it's time to go pick out a bike and start riding, right? No, not quite yet. There is still more preparation in order: riding gear. Most states require helmet use for at least some riders and several require eye protection, as well. A motorcycle jacket, pants, gloves, and boots will help you look the part and also protect you in the event of an unplanned dismount. Riding gear also helps keep you comfortable, which allows you to concentrate more on the road.

Now it's time to pick out a bike. But which one should you choose? The bike you buy depends entirely on who you are and for what you plan to use it. Ask yourself these questions:

- How will I use my bike? For sightseeing? Commuting? Sporting? Touring? Cruising? Exploring?
- What size do I need? Will I carry passengers or luggage? Will I be able to pick it up if I fall?
- Am I going to ride on city streets, suburban arterials, freeways, or back roads?
- Will my riding be short trips or long distances?
- How much am I willing to pay for insurance?

A first bike should be easy to ride, simple to maintain, and cheap to repair and insure. Spend your first couple years with a simple motorcycle to learn firsthand what you really want and need in a bike.

Having a license and a bike to ride is a great start and it is important you get out there and practice. However, it is not a bad idea to consider taking some advanced training to guide you in your evolution as a motorcycle rider. There is always more to learn, and as the Motorcycle Safety Foundation so aptly puts it, "The more you know, the better it gets."

Aspiring riders line up to take the first steps to two-wheel freedom at a riding school (opposite). Everyone has to reach the same basic standard before passing their test.

Basic Training

The Motorcycle Safety Foundation's Basic RiderCourse means just what it says, but what does it involve? Its main purpose is to provide you with the fundamental skills for your own road safety as you embark on your biking career. The BRC was devised to prepare novice riders for the street and reduce the number of crashes, injuries and fatalities for all riders—and it works.

Front brake does most of the stopping as weight transfers to the front tire under braking, so give it the most attention.

Throttle gives you go and slow, with useful engine braking on four strokes.

Rear brake is usually a much smaller, less powerful setup than the front. With weight transferred forwards under braking the back tire has less grip, so could lock-up.

Gear lever most commonly follows the one down, five up shift pattern.

Clutch control counts for a lot, and the CBT features lots of excercises to get it right.

You can take the BRC on your own bike or one provided by your training school Call 800-446-9227 to find a course near you. You will need to provide your own riding gear. This includes eye protection and a DOT-approved helmet, long pants and long sleeves, sturdy boots that cover your ankles and full-fingered gloves.

Remember to take your driver's license and your permit, if you have one. The instructor will want to check it before training begins. If you plan on riding your own bike in the course, you will need to show proof of insurance. Your motorcycle must pass a simple safety inspection.

By now, you'll be itching to get on with the business of riding, but first the classroom beckons for a look at what the BRC involves and a chat about risk, riding strategy and protective clothing. After breaking ground with preparation and attitude, the instructors will get to the good part: riding the bike. All the basics of riding will be discussed in the classroom before you even get a look at a live motorcycle. Subjects include rider posture, turning, shifting, and stopping. Add to that the street concepts of hazard detection, visibility, positioning, special riding situations, and alcohol. Once you understand basic skills and riding strategy, the instructors will guide you through cornering, surmounting obstacles, emergency braking, swerving, carrying passengers, and dealing with surface hazards. The classroom discussion primes you for the on-cycle instruction.

At last it's time to get down to riding. You'll master starting the bike, clutch control, stopping, dealing with other traffic, and low-speed maneuvers. All these drills teach the basic of straight-line riding, turning, shifting, and stopping.

Once you can handle the basics, the trainers will teach you cornering, emergency stopping, swerving,

and U-turns. All this is done in the safe confines of the "range," usually a concrete or asphalt parking lot marked out with cones and painted lines.

Your instructors, called "RiderCoaches," will help ensure that you get all the feedback and encouragement you need to succeed. Don't panic if things don't come easily, because coaches are well trained and experienced riders with a desire to turn out safe riders. They will give you as much advice and practice time as they can.

In the end, you'll put all the classroom discussion and the on-cycle exercises into practice and take your final tests. The knowledge test is 50 questions derived from the classroom discussion and requires a score of 40 correct to pass. The riding skill test is four drills that evaluate your ability to do low-speed U-turns, execute a swerve, stop quickly and use proper cornering technique. You will have practiced all the test exercises during the course. Twenty or fewer points deducted from your score is a passing score.

Provided you attended the entire course and passed your two tests, you'll be issued a completion card. This means you demonstrated the basic skills and knowledge necessary to ride on the street. Many states will waive any further tests and issue your motorcycle endorsement upon course completion. Others may still require a knowledge and/or skill test to earn your license. Either way, you will have earned the right to call yourself a motorcyclist. Get your license, take to the road, and practice what you have learned.

A BRC usually takes two to four days to complete, but don't be downhearted if you need to take it more than once. Everyone learns at different rates and, remember, your instructor wants to be sure that you're safe. Whether you are new to motorcycling or an old pro, the BRC is a definite must in your career as a rider.

The **knowledge** test

Even though you may have learned everything you need to know in your basic training course, most states require that you also pass a written or computer test to get your license. Think of this as another opportunity to show off your motorcycle knowledge and mental abilities.

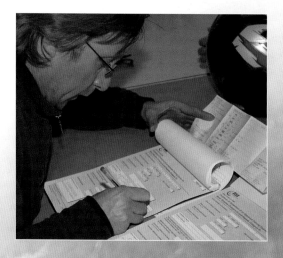

But don't be fooled. Even though operating a bike might seem like a big challenge at first, motorcycling is ultimately mental, and your local branch of government that provides the licenses understands that. When you sit down to take the test, you had better know what you're doing.

You'll be tested on preparation, protective riding gear, motorcycle controls, rider responsibility and awareness and conspicuity. You will also have to demonstrate your knowledge of proper positioning in traffic, techniques for riding safely and performing emergency maneuvers, defensive riding strategy and hazard detection, surface problems, carrying passengers, group riding, mechanical problems and alcohol impairment.

Most states base the knowledge test on the Motorcycle Safety Foundation's "Motorcycle Operator Manual," available at your state department of public safety, transportation, motor vehicles, or highway patrol.

The **skill** test

Now you're ready for the big one. Time to put everything you've learned to the test under the scrutiny of a state license examiner. Some states restrict bike size for minors, but no longer impose size restrictions on adults. You could take the test on a 125-cc commuter bike, then buy a bike as big as the 2294-cc Triumph Rocket III.

On your way to the exam station, you will be riding on your learner's permit and subject to permit rules. Provided everything goes as planned, you won't be required to obey all those restrictions on your way back!

The examiner will want to check your documents—license, permit, and training documents—and you'll need to have your state photo ID with you. This last item is required to discourage candidates from sending someone else along to take the test for them. Some exam stations test motorcyclists at specific times, so it is best to call ahead and schedule an appointment.

With the formalities out of the way, it's time to take to the road, in most cases an off-street test course designed by the Motorcycle Safety Foundation. Some states use an on-street format for the exam.

The examiner is looking for you to ride safely, sensibly, and confidently through a variety of maneuvers designed to measure your skill with the motorcycle. You'll have practiced all of these manuevers in your training course. If you chose not to get training, most state motorcycle manuals have diagrams of the test for review.

While the value of being able to navigate around little cones at low speeds may be debatable, the skills the examiners measure are not. Successful completion requires slow-machine control, turning, stopping, and swerving. Some tests require faster cornering maneuvers. If your jurisdiction uses an on-street test, you'll be outfitted with a two-way radio and the examiner will follow you in a car and give you instructions for 10 to 20 minutes.

Provided you manage to perform the various elements of the test competently, and don't make any dangerous or potentially dangerous mistakes (like dropping your bike), you'll pass and be able to kiss those permit restrictions goodbye. Congratulations.

Remember that passing means you've shown a minimum level of skill to ride safely. It doesn't automatically mean you're ready for passengers or a big, fast bike.

Don't let your newfound two-wheeled freedom go to your head—know your limitations. Riding is great fun, but you need practice and experience to achieve the skill level that truly defines the term "motorcyclist." If you keep your speed down, pay attention to your surroundings, and keep your bike in top shape, you're sure to enjoy a lifetime of motorcycling.

Advanced training

Advanced training has something to offer everyone—whether you've just passed your test, have been riding for years, or are returning to motorcycling after a break from it.

If the ink is barely dry on your bike license, you might be wondering why you should want to have even more instruction. After all, you've just successfully taken on a whole load of new knowledge and shown the world that you know what you're doing, thank you very much. But steep though the learning curve was from wobbly-wheeled novice in the BRC to confident, competent rider in the skill test, there's always more to learn beyond the bare basics of control that you had to show the examiner. Once you have a few miles under your belt, you can take the next step and become a better rider by taking an MSF Experienced RiderCourse.

Or if you're coming back into motorcycling after a few years away, you can gain an instant boost to your confidence on today's faster bikes and busier road systems by signing up for an ERC. Even riders who've been at it for years can benefit.

There are a few private advanced training organizations springing up, so there may be a course to better suit the level of skills you currently have. At the moment, there is little formal regulation of advanced training organizations. That's not to say that a private school is a fly-by-night operation, but pay attention to the recommendations of other riders, bike magazines, and dealers.

ERCs are generally conducted by the same institutions and taught by the same rider coaches that teach the basic courses. And while these advanced training sessions take place on the same closed-off parking lots as the basic courses, the exercises are tougher and the pace is quicker—plus, you ride your own motorcycle instead of a 125-cc training bike. The coaches are experts at observing good and bad habits and offering insight into developing your technique. They also rely on student experience and skill to help guide the class and learn new tricks themselves. In addition to helping hone riders' mental strategies, the ERC uses comprehensive drills to give riders practice in emergency stops, cornering skill and judgment, swerving, and superior motorcycle control. Many seasoned riders and motorcycle clubs take the experienced course every year or every other year to blow out the cobwebs.

Central to advanced training is self-observation, and learning to make the most of your mind and machine. An advanced course should help you hone your control techniques to corner, brake, and swerve better and safer, and make the optimum use of your limited attention. The more this stuff becomes second nature to you, the more fun you'll have on a bike.

Apart from the state and private training schools, many race tracks and racing clubs offer economical advanced training in various parts of the country. Your local law enforcement agency may offer training too.

With proper instruction, you can learn techniques in a day or two, which otherwise might take years for you to develop on your own. And once you've learned advanced techniques you'll use them every time you ride. View every ride as an opportunity to hone your skills and technique.

Advanced training on the road (above) involves accompanied rides where experienced instructors assess your riding. The California Superbike School (left) holds track-based training where the emphasis is on developing machine control.

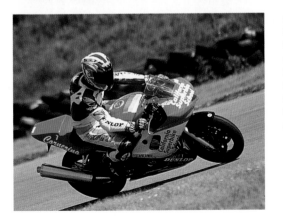

A student of the California Superbike School puts the theory into practice, developing skills on the track that will improve his road riding too. The right mix of road and track advanced training makes for more confident and safer riders.

Think you're fast? Explore the limits of your bike and your riding ability by going on a trackday, or guarantee improved skills by signing up for a race school. Plus you'll get to ride challenging and famous circuits without making the huge commitments of time and cash demanded by racing.

Trackdays and race school

Gloves *Choose race-style for adequate protection and good feel.*

Leathers *A good one-piece is best, a zip-together two-piece is the next choice.*

Knee sliders *Trackday heroics can be measured in how many pairs of sliders you get through. Most circuits frown on metal pucks.*

Boots *Good race boots are best for protection and feel.*

The popularity of trackdays has led to a burgeoning industry that offers events nationwide pretty much all year-round.

Apart from yourself and your bike, you'll need one-piece or good-quality zip-together two-piece leathers (see page 50), a helmet with a DOT and Snell stamp (page 48), gloves (page 54), and boots (page 56). You may be required to tape up lights, indicators, and mirrors. Most trackday organizers require you to show your driver's license when you sign on at an event, to prove that you've at least some idea of how to ride a bike. This is a condition imposed on them by their insurers. You'll be asked to fill out a waiver form to limit the liability of the organizers, stating that you understand the nature of the event and that you're fit to take part. Don't forget to check with your own insurers that your policy extends to trackdays. If it doesn't, arrange additional cover, just in case the worst happens.

At most trackdays, riders are divided into groups depending on ability, ranging from novice (slow) to advanced (close to race pace). Choose the group you reckon you'll be most comfortable in. If you find yourself running rings around everyone in the slow group, then have the organizers move you up. It's better that way than starting out in too quick a group, being unsettled by faster riders screaming past you, and having to haul yourself and your shattered ego down a class.

Before the track time begins, you'll be given a briefing to explain where the track goes and what the different signal flags mean. Start each session slowly and give your tires time to warm up. Most crashes happen on cold tires, where the rider gets a bit aggressive at the start of a session. Use the day's early sessions to learn where the track goes and the best lines through the turns.

Groups usually go out for 15 to 20 minutes at a time. Doesn't sound like long, but it's long enough when you're concentrating and exerting plenty of physical energy. The hardest part is waiting until it's your group's turn to go out again. Trackdays can be draining, so keep fluid levels up by drinking plenty of water and eating little and often—high-energy foods such as snack bars are ideal.

If you want to accelerate the learning curve, think about signing up for a race school. Structures vary, but most assign an instructor (usually a racer) to groups of roughly the same ability (typically no more than five riders, and sometimes one-to-one). A race school is the best way to work towards quick results on specific aspects of your riding, and you may not even need to use your own bike since some schools provide the machines.

Approached properly, trackdays and race schools will improve your machine control, which can only add to your riding skills and enjoyment. Check bike publications and the Internet or ask your local bike dealer for details of events. And be warned: trackdays are addictive....

Helmets

A helmet is the single most important piece of motorcycle clothing you will buy—and not just because they're often a legal requirement. The right lid, fitted correctly, could save your life in an accident. If you ever have to put a helmet to the test—and we hope you never do—you'll be glad you're wearing a good one.

There's no need to spend a fortune to get a helmet that will provide an adequate level of protection. All helmets sold in the US, except for fake "novelty" helmets, have to comply to a baseline standard to be legal for road use. More expensive helmets meet exactly the same standards as cheaper ones, the differences being in more complex construction, increased comfort, and the quality and complexity of finish, visor mechanism, vents, liner material, removable liners, and so on.

After the strap that holds your helmet on (usually a seatbelt-type or a pair of D-rings through which the strap passes), the next most important components are the outer shell and inner liner. Outer shells are usually injection-molded polycarbonate (normally, but not always, used at the lower end of the market) or a laminate of glass fiber, carbon fiber, and Kevlar. The outer shell is there to resist abrasion and penetration, and to distribute impact forces across a larger area.

The inner is molded polystyrene designed to deform on impact, absorbing the force of a blow. For this reason, helmets that have sustained an impact should be replaced, or at least inspected—they're designed to take only one hit. Inside the inner is a foam-backed cloth liner. This has no protective value and is there for comfort only. The helmet must fit your head evenly without excessive pressure at any point. If there is pressure, try another size or make. Many helmets have vents to allow cool air in and warm air out, which is intended to reduce fogging. There are anti-fog preparations and laminates available to help minimize this almost inevitable problem of full-face helmets. Laminates provide longer-term protection than sprays that have to be regularly applied.

Never set your helmet on its side; place it carefully on its base. Use only very mild detergents and polish on lids, since solvents can attack shells and visors. Never buy a second-hand helmet—you don't know its history and it could have been dropped. Some helmets are quieter than others, but none are so quiet as to prevent hearing damage from wind noise—so also consider ear plugs.

The DOT label on helmets (referring to compliance with Federal Motor Vehicle Safety Standard 218) is sometimes complimented by a Snell Memorial Foundation or American National Standards Institute decal, meaning it has been put to additional performance tests. Beware of cheap-looking helmets that don't bear the label—these are sold for novelty purposes only and are not street legal. Bicycle helmets, often used as inexpensive solutions for permit restrictions and for very young passengers, are not legal for use on motorcycles, either.

Plan to replace your helmet every four to five years, regardless of how well you've looked after it, because the materials that make up your lid degrade over time. And always replace scratched visors as soon as possible.

Full-face helmets provide the most protection.

Motocross lids make for urban cool on the road.

Scooter, retro, and classic riders often favor open-face.

Many excellent, high-tech man-made materials are now being used in motorcycle clothing. But when it comes to crash protection, particularly from abrasion, there's still nothing to top good old-fashioned leather—especially when those leathers have state-of-the-art armor built in. There are a nearly infinite number of styles and choices, so it pays to do your research and shop around to make sure your leathers will do what you hope they'll do. Some leathers cannot be sold as protective clothing—as opposed to merely fashion items—in Britain and Europe, unless their design and construction have passed a British or European Standard. There are no such requirements in the US, so buy your gear from a shop or manufacturer that specializes in motorcycle apparel. And remember, you get what you pay for, and good protection isn't cheap.

Leathers

All the colors, all the shapes, this Spyke suit's top level kit.

This time there are zippers right around the waist.

While leather is very good for sliding along in, it doesn't have much in-built impact protection. That's why it pays to have decent armor at likely impact points—shoulders, elbows, back, hips, and knees. Some cheap leathers (and indeed some more expensive ones) have foam padding in these areas. That isn't going to help much in a crash. Proper armor, designed to absorb some of the energy of an impact, will.

Armor is usually made of two or more materials—a harder outer layer made of dense foam or plastic, and a softer inner layer. The outer layer spreads the load across the inner, which cushions the impact. Decent armor finds the middle ground between too hard—which only serves to deflect the shock of impact directly to your body, and too soft, which will do the same.

As with the leathers that carry the armor, there are no standards for armor sold as protective equipment, so seek recommendations from the sources you trust most. For more detail on armor, see page 62.

With the object of getting decent leathers in mind, there's only one choice left—one piece or two piece? One-piece suits give instant racer chic, but unlike a two-piece you can't just slip the jacket off when you reach your destination. Two-piece suits usually zip together, and the farther around your waist that zipper extends, the better it will hold together in the event of a tumble.

One-piece suits are widely viewed as offering superior protection. That is not always the case—there are good and bad suits in each category. Look for good quality hide, double layers (panels should be sewn on rather than sewn in) and armor on impact points.

If your leathers get wet, let them dry out naturally, otherwise the material and stitching can weaken. Should they become dirty, clean them with a very mild detergent solution and, again, allow them to air dry. There are many leather treatments on the market, but some of them are better suited to horse saddles than bike suits. Use sparingly and don't soak the stitching with them, at the risk of weakening it. And don't be tempted to use waterproofing solutions on leather for the same reasons. Carry rain gear (page 58) to wear over your leathers when the clouds open up. Good leathers cost a lot but, just like a decent helmet, they're more than worth it. Looked after properly they will last and, more importantly, protect you for years. Only the colors and styling go out of date.

Fabric
jackets &
trousers

A fabric jacket can be as stylish as leathers.

Leather might provide the ultimate in crash protection, but other than wind protection, it struggles to keep out the other elements. That's where fabric jackets and pants come into their own. What's more, modern materials and armor mean they can run leathers a close second when things go badly.

There's a huge array of fabric clothing available, at all prices. What the clothing costs isn't always an indication of how water/wind/crash-proof it'll be, but features such as armor, thermal, and waterproof linings made of space-age materials and features like pockets and vents all tend to drive prices up.

Fit is all important. Jacket sleeves must be long enough so they don't ride up with arms outstretched; likewise the back and pant legs when you're crouched in riding position. If you expect to wear the jacket over winter layers or one-piece leathers, it has to be roomy, but ideally not so baggy as to flap around with the thermal liner removed on warmer days. Pants and jackets that zip together are preferable to those that don't, not only for warmth, but also to prevent them parting company and exposing your flesh in a crash. Adjustable straps on the collar, waist, wrists, elbows, and ankles help ensure the best fit. Flaps over zippers help keep wind and water out, and check that the fasteners nearest the waist and crotch are rubber-covered to prevent damage to tank paintwork.

Armor is fitted in many fabric jackets and pants, and is usually removable to allow the garments to be worn over leathers containing armor of their own. When you try on a jacket or pants, make sure that the armor isn't too free to move around. It needs to stay close to the areas it is designed to protect or else it won't be much use in a crash.

As with leathers, double stitching and layers are definite bonuses on impact points like elbows and posterior. Fabrics lack the durability of leather, so it's pretty much a foregone conclusion that you'll grind holes in them even in low-speed spills.

Most modern jackets and pants have a waterproof membrane under the outer layer—look for Gore-Tex and Sympatex labels. These fabrics keep moisture out while allowing sweat to escape.

So while decent fabric clothing should keep you warm and dry, it won't provide ultimate crash protection. But it's certainly better than simple nylon rain gear, which are very much a second line of defense on top of proper protective clothing.

Waist belt keeps wind from upper body. Good neck closure too.

Plenty of armor and upper-arm straps. Good.

Here's the basic setup. Look for decent armor, an effective neck closure, and straps at key points to make the suit fit you. Outer pockets need double closures to keep rain out, and your possessions in.

Lots of armor again. And a pocket for the mobile phone.

Here's a test you can conduct in the comparative safety of your own home. Place an obstacle in the middle of the floor—a kitchen or dining room chair should do it—and launch yourself at it in a comedy tumble-down style. In the ensuing melée, one thing will almost certainly happen. Your hands will make contact with the floor before any other part of your body does. This is a reaction that goes back to basic survival instincts.

Gloves

Consider that your hands shoot out first in a fall, and be assured that gloveless, T-shirted, shorts-wearing, trainer-shoed casual summer riders are cruising for much more than a bruising. It isn't called protective clothing for nothing, and after a decent helmet, proper gloves are the next most essential line of defense.

At their most basic, gloves must let you still feel the controls through their protective layers. Leather is great for this. It breaks in nicely and molds to the shape of your hands and their movement. Double-layer leather and stitched-in protection should be there at impact points—specifically, palms and knuckles. As with most bike clothing, high-tech materials are being used more extensively, such as Kevlar , Cordura, and Thinsulate for, variously, protection, weatherproofing, and insulation. Many modern gloves are a combination of leather and these high-tech fabrics. Some are made wholly from non-leather materials.

Look for Velcro wrist straps and tighten them up enough for the gloves to stay on your hands in the event of a tumble.

When buying gloves, it's a good idea to take along your leathers or jacket to check for fit over or under the cuffs.

As the seasons change, so will your glove requirements. In their better-made (and usually more expensive) forms, race and summer gloves offer optimal feel of controls and great crash protection but poor insulation from rain and cold weather. Waterproof and windproof but breathable gloves are now available for all-weather riding, and insulated gloves keep out the chill on the coldest days.

If your leather gloves do get wet, let them air dry rather than putting them on top of a radiator or in the airing cupboard.

Basic race-style glove, note knuckle protection and long wrist.

Short race glove. Good hand protection, elastic wrist.

Lots of carbon and Kevlar in these Spidis. Fine leather for good feel, but no wrist straps.

Double layers, over-and-under the wrist straps, loads of protective inserts. Plenty of protection for even the most paranoid.

Boots

Decent bike boots are an important part of your protective clothing wardrobe. As well as your foot, they should also protect the ankle and lower leg, which are particularly vulnerable.

Leather is still the most common material used in bike boots but, as with clothing, many high-tech fabrics are being used—and not just for the linings.

Race-style boots usually have impact protection in the shin, ankle, calf, and heel areas. Foam is the minimum to look for and additional armor, made from high-impact plastic for example, is a definite bonus. To prevent them flexing in a tumble, soles are often reinforced with metal or plastic inserts, which still allow the sole to give when the wearer is walking. Zip closures are usually concealed behind a Velcro flap to reduce the chances of their opening in an impact and the boot flying off.

Full-on race boots come with toe and calf sliders and most flex sufficiently to make walking around in them reasonably easy. However, there's a rule of thumb that says the more protective a boot, the less comfortable it is off the bike. Not always true, but you certainly wouldn't want to go on a nature ramble in motocross boots.

Touring-style boots offer more of a compromise. Many give good levels of protection with the added bonus of a degree of waterproofing, although some sport boots are now also available with this. Touring boots are usually pretty comfortable off the bike.

Winter boots go even further, offering insulation too. As with gloves, this is important for winter riding. Most of your body's heat is lost through the extremities. Apart from being uncomfortable, coldness can result in reduced concentration or worse, especially when the wind-chill factor is taken into consideration.

Most riders wind up with several pairs of boots to suit the seasons or the type of riding they're doing.

When choosing boots, take your riding suit or pants with you to ensure they zip up okay over your leathers or under your oversuit. Like gloves, boots should always be allowed to air dry to preserve the leather.

Above and below, the simple, clean lines of touring boots can conceal a multitude of weatherproof fabrics.

Motocross boots; very protective, but very stiff for everyday use.

Race boots provide optimum support for least weight.

Back in the bad old days, waterproof clothing meant waxed cotton. And it did a reasonable enough job for the speeds of the day, but it also required continual reproofing and was an absolute dirt magnet. It's still available, but unless you're on some kind of retro trip, you may like to consider something a bit more up-to-date.

Rain gear

Then there were PVC oversuits. They were waterproof (until they ripped along their welded seams), but the buildup of sweat on the inside, even on mild days, could make you as wet as the rain you were trying to keep out.

Nylon is a popular material for rain gear and has the advantage of folding down small so they can be carried easily, often in an small fanny pack.

Today, though, modern synthetics allow rainsuits to pull off that neat trick of being waterproof and breathable at the same time; a real bonus on warm days or when riding any distance. Some suits are lined for additional protection from the cold. Many feature reflective material to boost your visibility at night.

Check that seams are taped on the inside to stop water seeping through. Zippers should also have Velcro flaps to prevent water getting in through the closures. And these closures should open sufficiently wide to allow you to get into the suit at the side of the road once the heavens have opened. Choose a suit large enough to go over your usual riding gear, and make sure it's big enough not to restrict your riding position when it's on, but not so big as to flap around like a gigantic sail on the move. Velcro ankle, wrist, and neck closures help to fit the suit snugly to your body and prevent water entering through these key areas.

Waterproof overboots and gloves are also available and are worth it if you think you're going to get caught out in the weather while wearing your summer gear. They fold down so small that they take up next to no space under your bike's seat.

Waterproof suits can carry armor too and boast many features of their less rain-stopping equivalents. As with any bike clothing, look for good fit.

Handy nylon one-piece can be carried in integral fanny pack 'til needed.

Thermals

Cold can be one of the rider's biggest enemies. Once you get chilly, your concentration starts to wander and accidents can happen. Even when the weather's just above zero degrees, wind chill can take the temperature you're enduring well down into the negative numbers. Apart from all that, it's just downright miserable, and biking's meant to be fun. But with the right gear, year-round riding needn't be a freezing chore.

Just make sure you take this beauty off before going into the bank.

Face and neck protector.

Dickie to cover neck and chest.

Thermal fleece is something you'll be grateful for.

Fingers get cold first without thermal gloves.

Balaclava extends to upper body.

Thermal pants—forget style, it's keeping warm that counts. Thermals make a huge difference in cold weather.

You could raid grandpa's underwear drawer for a pair of long johns and long-sleeved vest, because they'll serve you pretty well. Thermal underwear is available in most clothing chain stores at reasonable prices. More specialized thermals can be found in skiing and outdoor shops too.

Natural materials work well until they get wet, either from sweat or rain, when they tend to hold on to the moisture and take a long time to dry out. That's when cold can set in again. Silk is lighter and thinner than cotton or wool, so it tends to work better in this respect. Full synthetics tend to let body heat build up and up, which can be pretty uncomfortable too. One other problem is that synthetics often cause worse abrasions than natural fabrics in the event of a tumble.

Bike clothing manufacturers are wise to the problems and offer a variety of solutions, some of which combine natural and synthetic materials. These allow you to keep warm or cool as required, wicking sweat away from the body in the process.

A thermal neck warmer is a real boon on colder days, filling the vulnerable gap between jacket collar and helmet. A thin balaclava under your helmet is a great help too. As for the other extremities most prone to heat loss, thermal socks and inner gloves are indispensable.

Thermal clothing might just seem like another layer of protection to struggle in and out of, but on long cold rides, you'll be glad you bothered. And when thermals just don't cut it during your cold-weather riding, consider electric clothing, available from specialty motorcycle apparel manufacturers.

Armor

Leathers and man-made fabric suits provide varying degrees of abrasion protection, but neither offers the rider much impact protection. That's where armor comes into play. It can make the difference between serious injury and walking away from a tumble.

Highly protective Knox back protector covering shoulder, spine, and kidney areas. Straps go over shoulders and protector is further secured by Velcro waist belt.

Simple foam padding provides little if any protection. The most it does is to make suits more comfortable. Proper armor varies in hardness. Too unforgiving, and it transfers the shock of impact directly to the body. Too soft and the same thing happens. Good armor lies between these extremes and often has harder (outer) and softer (inner) elements, because it needs to take the initial impact, then deform to soften the blow as much as it can. It's very similar to what happens with a helmet (see page 48), where the hard outer takes the initial whack and prevents penetration of objects, and the soft, deformable inner cushions the impact. In theory, then, the inside of the lid quickly slows the rider's head to a stop, rather than the sudden contact with the ground.

Armor sold as protective equipment is not required to meet any national standard, just as with leathers.

Read up and solicit reviews from friends, dealers, and other sources you trust to find armor you'll be confident wearing on the street. Good armor is designed to pass as little as 30 percent of the force of an impact. As with helmets, replace any armor that's taken a significant impact in a crash. That's fairly simple on most riding suits, since it's held in Velcro-fastened pockets in the lining.

Check that armor is in the right place on any suit you're thinking of buying—not just where it's located (knees, hips, elbows, shoulders, and back), but also how it fits to your body.

Many riders use a separate back protector to give extra peace of mind. For comfort, you'll need to remove the one in your suit, if it has one. First developed for the race track, back protectors have saved many riders from severe injury.

State-of-the-art armor inserts

Above and right, motocross armor

Insurance

Any bike used or kept on the road has to be insured, not least because you need to show a current insurance policy to register your motorcycle. And even if you're keeping your bike off the road, perhaps for winter, you'll probably want theft coverage at least.

There are four main types of insurance coverage: liability, collision, comprehensive, and uninsured/underinsured. Cost rises in line with the level of coverage.

Liability is the basic legal minimum insurance required in most states to get you on the road. If you cause a crash, it covers injury to other people and damage to their property. It doesn't cover injury or damage to you or your bike and fire and theft are excluded.

Collision is optional insurance used to cover damage to your bike in a crash. This type of coverage sometimes includes your helmet and leathers, too. Comprehensive is also optional and provides protection against things like fire, theft, or flood damage.

Uninsured and underinsured motorist coverage protects you from injury and property damage costs in the event you have a tussle with a driver who lacks insurance or sufficient insurance. Many states require motorists to carry this type of coverage, but make not all require it of motorcycle riders.

Insurance companies look at a variety of factors in calculating your premium, or even to decide if they want to cover you at all. Your age, how long you've held a full license, occupation, address, any traffic convictions, previous claims, where the bike will be kept and, of course, the type of bike—all these factors have a bearing on how much your insurance coverage will cost.

The cost of insurance tends to drop at the ages of 21, 25, and 35. A 19-year-old pop musician with a Suzuki GSX-R1000, no garage, a reckless driving conviction, who has held a license for only one year and lives in the inner city, is unlikely to find an insurer willing to cover him or her. Even if an insurer will, the premium is likely to be prohibitively expensive. At the other extreme, a 55-year-old suburban parish priest with a commuter bike, a garage, and a clean license for 35 years, is likely to have an easier time of it.

Most riders fall between these extremes of course, and there is much you can do to reduce your premium so it pays to shop around. Insurance policies have a deductible, an initial amount of any claim you agree to pay yourself. If you agree to pay a higher deductible, your insurer will reduce the premium. Similarly, you can reduce your premium by garaging your bike, fitting an approved alarm or immobilizer, and taking a rider training course. It's worth taking all the anti-theft precautions that you can. Insurers often refuse theft coverage to people who've had machines stolen when they eventually get their replacement bikes.

A good driver discount can make a huge difference to your premium—up to 50 percent if you can maintain a clean insurance and driving record. Many states and insurance companies provide a rate reduction for riders who have completed a rider training course.

Above all, remember to play it straight with your insurer. If you make any major modifications to your bike, you must tell them or they could refuse to pay out on a claim. And they do keep a register of claims and investigate any dubious claims vigorously.

Most important of all, make sure you can get insurance coverage for the bike you want before committing to buying it. If you can't, all's not lost. Go for a bike in a lower insurance group that you can get cover for (bikes are graded according to type, performance, and how attractive they are to thieves) and do your best to build a good insurance record.

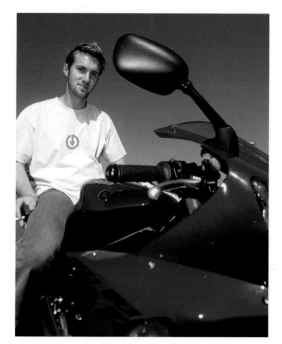

Bad: young, inner-city, big bike, expensive to insure.

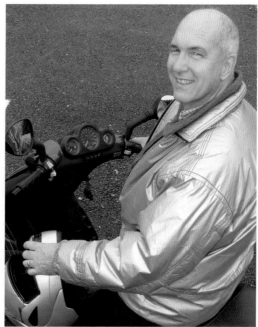

Good: old, small bike, more no-claims than nostril hairs!

Both ends of the risk scale as perceived by the insurance companies. Of course the truth lies somewhere between...

Security

Bike theft statistics make pretty depressing reading. Motorcycles are often stolen and stripped for parts—a lucrative business for the savvy bike thief. Precious few bikes are ever recovered. Physical security of machines is not high on bike manufacturers' list of priorities. The best you can expect as standard on most bikes is a steering lock on the ignition barrel incapable of withstanding anything more than a half-hearted attempt with a screwdriver. A sharp tug on the bars is enough to pop some. So that's the bad news. But take heart—there's still plenty you can do to reduce the chances of becoming part of the statistics.

U-locks and cables can often be stored under the seat.

If you're able to park your bike where you can see it while you go about your business, so much the better. This is rarely practical, though, so you'll need additional protection.

Always use a lock of some sort, no matter how short a time you're leaving your bike unattended. A disc lock is easy to carry and provides some amount of visible deterrent, hopefully enough to put off casual joyriders while you step into the store for a newspaper. But it won't stop more determined thieves from lifting your bike into a van.

A U-lock is bulkier and less easy to carry, but provides a similar level of security by passing through the brake discs at the fork legs to prevent the bike from being wheeled away. Some are large enough, or come with a cable, to secure the bike to another machine or an immovable object, such as a street light. Many modern bikes have a space under the seat for a U-lock, or there are carrying brackets that mount behind the license plate or on the frame.

The next step up is a high-quality lock and chain that will allow you to secure the bike to an immovable object. But while they provide a higher level of security, the larger they are, the more difficult they are to carry. They can be strapped in a bag on the passenger seat or carried in a tank bag or panniers, but for safety's sake don't be tempted to carry a lock and chain around your waist or over your shoulder.

When locking up, take care not to thread the chain through a part of the bike that can be easily removed, such as a footrest hanger, otherwise you

might come back to the bike to find yourself with no more than a solidly secured brake pedal. And if locking one of the wheels to the immovable object, be sure to wrap the chain around the rim rather than one of the spokes. Don't leave so much slack in the chain that its links (or the lock itself) can reach the ground, where they'll be all the easier for a thief to attack with a hammer.

While an alarm should be enough to put off a casual thief, it can't stop your bike from being lifted into a van. Neither can an immobilizer, but it can stop it from being ridden away. In some areas the use of an alarm or security device means a discount on your insurance premiums—if you have one that's on your insurance company's approved list of alarms and immobilizers. And because electronic security devices usually self-arm when you park the bike, they're one part of your security routine you won't forget. Sadly, though, most people ignore the screeches and bleeps of vehicle alarms these days, so you'll need to employ some form of physical security too.

Where you park is as important as what you do once you've parked. Busy, well-lit areas are best—even the most brazen thieves prefer a little privacy.

Be aware that thieves often follow their targets to see where they're going to park or where they live. Don't get paranoid. But if you suspect you're being tailed, there's no harm in going around the block one more time just to be sure.

When you're parking at work, try to arrange for you and a colleague to lock your bikes together. If

Getting heavy duty with big gauge chain and lock.

enough of you ride to work, your employers might agree to let you use part of a warehouse to park in, or fit ground anchors in the car park for your bikes. And make the security staff aware of your bike, then at least they'll know if the person taking an interest in the machine isn't you.

Some cities cement bike anchors into the ground. Use them whenever possible.

If your only option is to park outside, you might want to consider using a bike cover, which at least hides the bike from casual prying eyes. The more weathered and knackered the cover looks, the better. There could be any old junker under there.

All the advice on parking when you're out also applies at home, if you don't have the luxury of a shed or garage. If you have a backyard, park your bike there in preference to out front.

The safest place to store your bike is a secure shed or garage, and it may be a condition of your insurance that it's locked up at night. It's best to put your bike away as soon as you get home, and don't spend ages warming it up outside your house before you go out. Maintenance and cleaning are best done out of view too, or done quickly. And don't advertise the fact that you're a bike fan by plastering your garage or shed doors with bike stickers.

Fit a ground anchor in your shed or garage. Position it so it's difficult for a thief to access when

the bike's parked and thread the chain through the frame or swingarm and back wheel rather than through the front. Again, make sure the chain is taut enough to be clear of the floor and the lock is positioned so that it can't be pulled to the ground and smacked with a hammer.

Make your garage or shed doors secure too. Some metal garage doors are as easy to pop open as a can of beer. Fit extra deadbolts, but not to the extent of advertising the fact that there's something worth taking in there. Additional locks are best fitted on the inside of the door, where possible.

If your garage is adjacent to the house, and you have an alarm system, consider extending it to the garage. Should your garage or shed have electricity on a house circuit, you could use a cheap baby monitor for extra peace of mind.

No one likes talking about bike theft, but security is as essential to the motorcyclist as decent riding gear. Just ask anyone who's been unfortunate enough to lose a bike to a thief.

Remember, the biggest threat of theft comes not from the casual thief or joy rider, but the professional thief, many of whom steal to order. Do what you can to put both classes of scum out of business.

As almost three-quarters of stolen bikes are broken up to be sold for parts, there's one more security precaution that might put potential thieves off—marking your bike with an engraver. Engraving various parts with your name and phone number makes the stolen parts easier to trace. Some European systems use numbers or microchips stamped on to various bike components. These codes are unique to each owner, which allows the owner's name and address to be traced through a database when the stolen parts are found by the police. European police have scanners to read microchip tags, and tagging can provide the law with the evidence to convict bike thieves. Sadly, this technology is not available in the US. Yet.

This is one area of security where many manufacturers are beginning to do more for bike owners, even if these companies are still woefully lax on physical security. Many new bikes in Europe come with Datatag or similar as standard. Honda is using a marking system called Smart Water in some countries. The company has also introduced a concept called HISS (Honda Ignition Security System), a type of immobilizer that will only allow the bike to be started with the correct key. While we have this for four-wheeled vehicles in the US, we've yet to see it for motorcycles.

You may be able to buy a kit from your dealer and mark key components yourself, placing the sticker that comes with the kit on the screen or top of the tank to advertise that you've done it.

Don't become paranoid obsessive about bike security but be wary. Take as many steps as you reasonably can to protect your bike. Above all, use the best quality gear (do your research, shop around, solicit input from other riders on new products, or ask the advice of your local police theft unit and/or insurance company). With a little care and common sense, you can put bike theft lower down your list of worries.

One last thing: we can all do our part to stop theft by not buying bikes or parts we suspect to be stolen. Take away the demand and the supply will dwindle.

Keep your garage secure, but do it with discreet, internal locks like these (above) so as not to advertise what you've got.

Security is getting smarter, but so are thieves.

Fit an alarm/immobilizer as a first-line deterrent.

Luggage

When you're riding long distances, luggage storage is particularly valuable. There are two types available—hard and soft.

Tank bag mounts either by magnets or straps or a combination of both. Some have a holder that can be left mounted on the tank.

TRIUMPH

Ventura Bike Pac can be used as a backpack off the bike. This is better than a conventional backpack as you don't have to carry weight on your back while riding.

B-Bag mounts over the passenger seat. Design means some weight can be carried lower down.

Frank Thomas Cargo hard luggage is favored by some for its durability. Less easy to store off the bike, however.

Hard luggage is available as an option from some bike manufacturers and there is a healthy aftermarket making hard-shelled panniers and top cases. Some are available color-matched to your bike's paint scheme. The units are mounted on frames bolted to the bike and can be removed when you arrive at your destination. Most are lockable for limited security when you stop en route.

Soft luggage offers a bit more flexibility than hard luggage, in that it can be easily moved from bike to bike and doesn't need bolted-on framework, which can look unsightly when hard cases are removed.

There are various types of soft luggage. Tank bags have magnetic bases to attach them to the fuel tank, with straps for additional security or for using on plastic tanks. Some are expandable by means of an elaborate system of fabric and zippers. Others have straps and double as backpacks. Clear panels on top allow you to refer to maps or directions.

Throw-over panniers attach over the seat by a system of straps and laces. Some are shaped to accommodate the kicked-up pipes of sportbikes. There are tail packs too, which use bungee cords to attach to the passenger seat. Others mount on racks at the back of the bike. Panniers and tail packs are often expandable. The better soft luggage comes with rain covers that look like gigantic shower caps.

There are two main things to remember with luggage. The first is to ensure that it's securely mounted and doesn't hamper operation of the bike. Your trip will come to an unscheduled and unpleasant stop if soft panniers, for example, find their way into the back wheel. It's also surprising how much heat exhaust cans generate, enough to set panniers and their contents smoldering.

The second thing to remember is that you shouldn't overload luggage. Too much weight wrongly distributed will upset the handling of your bike. Your owner's manual will tell you how much can be safely carried. At a more basic level, cram too much into the bags and there's a chance they'll burst open. But if you don't mind airing your dirty clothes on the highway, then that's up to you.

Throw-over soft panniers These are from Triumph. Straps and bungee cords hold them on. Note how they're shaped so as not to touch the kicked-up pipes.

Gadgets

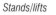

We're not talking here about simple customizing. Instead, we're interested in more handy accessories than Live-to-Ride bolt-ons, tinted headlamp covers, anodized bolts, and myriad other accessories that get in between the useful pages of so many accessory catalogs. The engine and chassis sections of this book look at the key items you might consider in those departments, so in the next couple of pages we'll turn our attentions to those items that will improve your biking life in more general and useful ways.

Stands/lifts

Few bikes come with center stands these days. They're options on some and almost a religious no-no on others, particularly sportbikes. Center stands make work on a bike easy where wheel removal is required (albeit with the assistance of bottle jacks and arbitrary bits of wood for the front), but in their absence, rear/front stands make sense.

Rear stands raise the back wheel off the floor by holding the swingarm or rear wheel spindle, while front stands raise the forks to bring the front wheel clear. Others, meanwhile, sit under the bottom yoke to hold the bike up in the absence of the front end.

Other stands are available to go under the engine and lift the whole bike up. Going the whole distance, you can buy a hydraulic lift to bring your bike close to eye level for maintenance.

Intercoms "Hello, hello, are you there? Go ahead, Houston. Did you see that guy? Are we there yet? Slow down. Speed up. Scream if you want to go faster." Yes, intercoms are endless fun and make riding more sociable. And when the novelty pales, you can always unplug them.

Tank protectors
These handy little items don't cost much, but spare your tank's finish from the worst your jacket or leathers have to inflict. Depending on the tolerance of your taste, you can choose clear or self-colored to something with silicone breasts on. But they all work the same.

Battery chargers
If your bike's going to be laid up for any length of time, and there's power in your garage, buy a trickle charger to keep your battery up to power. Otherwise it'll be dead and useless come springtime.

Fasteners
By all means use aftermarket alloy fasteners where they don't compromise structural integrity or come under extreme pressure—for example, holding on brake calipers. They save weight, look great, and corrode more slowly than some badly plated original equipment stuff.

Aftermarket bodywork, mirrors, indicators, levers
The first parts to take the flak in a tumble are also highly expensive. If you aren't a stickler for originality, a healthy aftermarket provides more affordable options. Bodywork, mirrors, indicators, and levers are all available in varying quality, but almost always at lower prices than original parts from a dealer. Track bike addicts have no qualms about using this stuff, because it mostly works. Hugger (above) is a useful bolt-on that stops road dirt and water from being flung at the rear shock by the back wheel.

Tire pressure gauges
As anyone who's struggled with gas station air lines and gauges will attest (see Tires), they were designed by an anti-biking devil who laughs diabolically as your money runs out. A foot pump and a decent analog or digital gauge are much better bets to keep pressure readings right on.

3

Know your motorcycle

Tires

You aren't going anywhere without tires, and they're arguably the most important parts of a motorcycle, with some of the toughest jobs to do. The rear transmits the power to the ground, while both have a huge part to play in the handling of the bike, offering grip in the turns as well as in a straight line. This grip is also vital for efficient braking.

Fit the correct tires for your bike and type of the riding you do—and don't be tempted to mix and match brands or types.

Tires do plenty for us and ask for little in return. Don't take them for granted. Check every week that they're at your bike manufacturer's recommended pressures. Do this when they're cold. Your machine manual will tell you the correct pressures for solo, passenger, and riding with luggage.

Under-inflation accelerates wear, ruins handling, raises fuel consumption, and lowers top speed. Over-inflation makes the ride less comfortable and reduces the size of the patch of tire in contact with the road, upsetting handling. It can also lead to premature wear. So it pays to get tire pressures right, although anyone who's ever struggled to inflate their bike tires with a gas station air line will understand why people neglect them. Buy a footpump and a decent tire pressure gauge—and don't trust the cheap plastic item on top of most footpumps.

Remember to replace the valve caps. At higher speeds, centrifugal forces can have the same effect on a valve stem as putting your finger on it. The only thing stopping the air escaping is the valve cap. Metal ones with rubber seals inside are best for motorcycle applications.

Wear indicators—little raised ridges across and in the bottom of the tread grooves—show when your tires have reached the end of the manufacturer's recommended safe wear limit. Little arrows or the letters TWI (tread wear indicator) at the "shoulder" or top of the tire wall indicate the grooves they're in.

Occasionally, other damage such as punctures or tears might mean they need to be changed before they wear out. It's a good idea before every ride to check for punctures and tears, or any foreign objects such as glass or nails stuck in the tread. There is another thing that might lead to early replacement, especially if your regular riding doesn't feature many corners. That's when the tires square off—the tires lose their semi-circular profile at the center of the tread.

Fit the correct type of tires to your bike, look after them and they'll look after you.

Tire types

There are three main tire types—crossply, bias-belted, and radial. These days crossplies are mainly found on lighter, slower bikes, although they are available with up to a 130mph-plus rating for some bikes. Bias-belts were developed for the emerging class of superbikes in the 1970s and are still fairly popular. But radials are the most modern construction.

As well as being the most modern, radial construction is fast becoming the most popular tire type—you'll find nothing else on sportbikes. Radials almost always run without inner tubes.

In a crossply, the plies that make up the carcass cross the circumference at around 25–35 degrees and are layered to crisscross each other. A bias-belted tire has additional plies under the crown (the treaded rubber part) to prevent centrifugal expansion under load and slow wear.

The plies in a radial tire run at 90 degrees across the circumference, with what are called crown plies running at more oblique angles to maintain the profile, a bit like the older bias belts do.

Apart from the carcass, there are elements common to all tires. The bead is made from wire and holds the tire to the rim. The bead filler is a rubber insert that helps strengthen the sidewall—the area between the bead and the crown, which is the treaded rubber section. The shoulder is where the sidewall meets the crown.

Tires come in different compounds of rubber that are invariably a compromise between grip and longevity. Tourer riders will want longevity over ultra-grip, while the sportbike rider seeking to make the most of the bike's handling will want grip above anything else. Some tires even have multiple compounds on the crown—hard and long-wearing in the middle, softer on the edges for the turns.

Although it's important, compound is not the single most vital aspect of a tire. It's the carcass that's the busiest part of the tire. A mix of various synthetic fibers and steel wires, it controls the shape of the tire, how it deflects and flexes, and the temperature at which it runs.

A modern radial tire. Michelin uses special Delta construction for stability.

Typical road construction. Tread pattern is optimized for water clearance, ensuring grip in wet and dry conditions.

A radial tire showing the different plies.

Bias belted tire.

Buying, choosing & fitting tires

Rear tires usually wear out before fronts because that's where all the power is transmitted. Don't be tempted to mix and match tire types or use one from a different manufacturer. They're designed and tested in pairs. If your tires are tubed, fit a new inner tube too. Some radials can be fitted with tubes, but check with the manufacturer's recommendations. And always fit tires of the correct load and speed ratings for your bike.

Don't buy oversize (that's wider) tires for your bike thinking they'll give more grip. They won't, and there could be clearance problems with the swingarm or other chassis components, which will upset the handling. Likewise, an undersize tire will have too flat a profile when fitted.

The Haynes workshop manual for your bike gives instructions on changing tires, but if you don't feel up to the job, or your tires are tubeless and you don't have access to a compressed air line, you might want to entrust the job to a shop. Tires are directional, and the direction of rotation is indicated by an arrow on the sidewall. They must be mounted the right way forward.

It's a good idea to have new valves installed in the rims when having new tubeless tires fitted, since the rubber bodies can harden and fail. Short valve stems minimize the problems of centrifugal force described in the first part of this chapter.

Some makes of tires have colored dots to indicate the lightest part of the tire and the mounter must position this adjacent to the valve.

Tire mounting lubricant or soapy water is used to clean the bead and help it seal. With the stem core of the valve removed, the tire is inflated to about 50psi until the bead seats. The core is then refitted and the tire inflated to operating pressure. Control lines concentric with the bead show if the tire is evenly seated to the bead. If not, the tire is deflated and the process repeated.

The wheel is then balanced, stick-on weights being put opposite the point the tire always stops at until the wheel stops randomly when spun. Unbalanced wheels upset handling and tire wear is accelerated.

Puncture repair with mushroom-type plugs is possible on some tubeless tires, depending on the severity of the hole. Puncture repair is not possible when the damage is on the sidewall rather than the tread. Different countries have different regulations, and manufacturers make their own recommendations. For safety reasons, these are best adhered to. Don't be tempted to patch punctured tubes—use new ones instead. Tubed tire punctures, where fixable, should be repaired by vulcanization to prevent moisture from attacking the carcass.

New tires should be gently broken in for the first 100 miles or so. The tread of new tires is smooth and manufacturing compounds make it slippery. So no heavy braking, hard acceleration or cornering until the tires are broken in.

If in doubt, hammer it out, or in. Mechanic puts the rear spindle back in.

Wheel balancing is essential, especially for the front tire. A good mounter will use a dynamic machine to do this for you.

Engine **types**

There are plenty of engine configurations in current production, but they all work in one of two ways—as two-strokes or four-strokes. The strokes refer to the number of times the piston moves up and down the bore in each combustion cycle. And that tells you a lot about the characteristics of the engine and its mechanical makeup.

The four-stroke process in four easy steps; suck, squeeze, bang, blow. Also known as the Otto cycle. It's powered most bikes of the last 100 years.

Induction: as the piston descends the inlet valve opens, allowing the fuel/air mixture to be drawn directly into the combustion chamber.

Compression: the piston starts to ascend and the inlet valve closes. The mixture is compressed as the piston rises.

Ignition: the spark plug ignites the compressed mixture, forcing the piston down the bore.

Exhaust: the exhaust valve opens to allow the burned gases to be expelled through the exhaust port as the piston rises.

A combustion cycle consists of induction (air and fuel in), compression (squeezing the mixture), ignition (setting it alight), and exhaust (getting the spent gases out). This is the same no matter how many strokes an engine is. Helpfully, the stages are pretty self-explanatory.

Air and fuel are drawn into the combustion chamber during induction, squashed in compression, ignited and burned during ignition (sometimes called power), and removed from the combustion chamber during exhaust. That's the process the engine has to go through in order to covert the chemical energy in gas into something we can use to make our bike move.

There are several differences between two- and four-stroke engines, but the most apparent is how they control the flow of gas in and out of the combustion chamber.

A four-stroke

The four-stroke gets its name because it takes four strokes to complete one combustion cycle. At the start of the cycle, the piston is at TDC (top dead center—as far up the bore as it can travel), and the valves are shut. As the crankshaft turns, the piston drops down the bore and the inlet valve opens, allowing fresh fuel and air mixture into the cylinder.

As the piston reaches BDC (bottom dead center—as far down the bore as possible), the inlet valve closes, trapping the mixture in the cylinder. That is the induction stroke.

As the crankshaft continues to rotate, it now starts to push the piston back up the bore towards TDC. Since all the valves are shut, sealing the cylinder, the air/fuel mixture has nowhere to go and gets compressed more and more until the piston is again at TDC. The piston has now done two strokes, one down the bore and one back up, and the crankshaft has turned through one revolution.

With the mixture squashed in the small space above the piston, it's ready to ignite—so the spark plug sparks and starts a fire in the mixture, causing it to expand rapidly and push forcibly on all the surfaces. As our piston is the only thing that can move, the high pressure in the cylinder pushes the piston back down the bore until it reaches BDC and can't be pushed any farther. This is the end of the ignition/power stoke.

All that is required now is to empty the burned gas from the cylinder. At this point, the exhaust valve opens and the high-pressure gas starts to make its way past the exhaust valve and into the exhaust pipe. This is helped by the piston, which is coming up the bore towards TDC, driving the gas out of the cylinder.

Once it reaches TDC, the exhaust valve closes and the inlet valve opens ready to start the next combustion cycle. In all, the piston has moved in the bore four times and the crankshaft has rotated twice.

That's the simplified view of the four-stroke, although in fact the valves are timed so that the exhaust stays open briefly as the inlet opens to admit the fresh charge, the waste gases helping to draw in the next fresh mixture charge.

Two-strokes

A two-stroke goes through the same combustion cycle as a four-stroke, but in half the time. A two-stroke doesn't have valves in the top of the combustion chamber. Instead, it has holes (ports) in the cylinder wall, which are covered and uncovered by the piston as it rises and falls. By setting the ports at different levels, it's possible to cover and uncover them at the correct times in the induction and ignition cycles.

It's also important to know that two-strokes carry their lubrication in the air/fuel mixture, either pumped in from a separate tank to the crankcases to mix with the fuel or pre-mixed in the fuel tank. This mixture is held in the crankcase, underneath the piston before it enters the cylinder. The oil content in the mixture lubricates the crankshaft and connecting rod bearings, and the rise and fall of the piston is used to pump the air/fuel mixture into the cylinder.

With the piston at BDC both the inlet and exhaust ports are uncovered, and fresh mixture is displaced into the cylinder through the inlet port. As the piston rises, it first covers the inlet port, stopping any more mixture from entering the cylinder and completing induction. As the piston rises farther, it also covers the exhaust port to seal the cylinder, and compression starts to take place.

The mixture is fully compressed when the piston reaches TDC, and in one movement the two-stroke has completed both induction and compression. The four-stroke's piston has to move twice to do this.

The spark plug now ignites the mixture to give us the power stroke. The piston is then forced back down the bore by the expanding gas until it uncovers the exhaust port. At this point the pressure of the burned gas starts to escape into the exhaust pipe, completing both ignition/power and exhaust in one more stroke.

In all, the piston has gone up and down the bore once, but has completed all four parts of the combustion process. The crankshaft has gone around only once too. Rather than leave our piston waiting, we should explain that as it travels a little farther down it uncovers the inlet port again, allowing fresh mixture to enter the cylinder.

At this point, exhaust gas will still be flowing out through the exhaust port while fresh mixture enters the cylinder via a process called scavenging. The big advantages of a two-stroke are that you get a power stroke for every crank revolution and there are fewer moving parts, which makes the engine cheaper and easier to build. The drawback is they aren't as efficient or economical as four-strokes.

Induction of fresh mixture into crankcase and *compression* of existing mixture in combustion chamber.

Ignition and exhaust of existing mixture in combustion chamber, and transfer of fresh mixture to combustion chamber.

Engine layout

As well as being two- or four-stroke, engines vary in their layout. The simplest is a single-cylinder engine, commonly found in anything from small commuter bikes to thumping supermotos. Usually, the cylinder points straight up and sits on top of the crankcases and gearbox. You'll also find singles with their cylinder pointing forwards or at an angle (inclined). But singles are just the start of what's possible.

Two-stroke single

Four-stroke V-twin

Four-stroke opposed twin

Two-stroke V-twin

Four-stroke inline triple

Four-stroke inline four Honda CBR900RR is one of the finest examples of this layout.

The next stage up from a single is to put two cylinders next to each other and make a parallel twin. This has several advantages because now there are two of everything. Two cylinders mean there is twice as much room to burn fuel, and gives the potential to have twice as many power strokes per crank revolution. But because we need only one crank and one gearbox, the engine doesn't have to be twice the physical size, which is an important factor as far as bikes are concerned.

As well as parallel twins, you'll also see 45-, 60-, 70-, and 90-degree V-twins, or opposed twins (BMW Boxers, for example) where the cylinders point in opposite directions. Each has slight advantages and disadvantages over the other but, in general, the most common twins at the moment are V-twins, made popular by Ducati and Harley-Davidson.

The engine layout you're most likely to see these days is the inline four, which is essentially two parallel twins side by side, albeit with a co-joined crank. Inline fours can be found in capacities from 250cc to 1400cc and are widely used since they balance compactness with the ability to make large amounts of power. They also run smoothly because of their configuration and can rev higher, which makes them easy to tune and good for everyday riding. Vibration is quite a big concern on singles and parallel twins. This problem is normally reduced with balancer shafts, although with the right engine layout these are almost unnecessary.

Finally there are a collection of other configurations such as V4s (used by Honda in its VFR sport tourer street and race bikes), V6s, opposed fours, triples, and even inline sixes, although you won't see many of those around. We're likely to see a host of new configurations in the future as technology developed in GP racing makes its way into road bikes. These could include V5s (Honda's 2002 four-stroke GP bike) and V3s, which are being raced or developed at the moment.

Racing has always improved the breed, and soon we'll be taking our pleasure on a new class of thoroughbred.

Four-stroke V4 is a Honda favorite, this is a VFR800FI.

Four-stroke single easiest and cheapest four-stroke to manufacture for reliable performance.

Four-stroke parallel twin backbone of the old British bike industry, finds favor in OHC form today.

Transmission

All the power being generated by your engine has to find its way to the back wheel as efficiently as possible. And that's the job of the transmission or drive train. There are four main elements here—primary drive, clutch, gearbox, and final drive.

Cross-section of a clutch

Torque — Friction plate — Plain plate — Pressure plate — Clutch spring — Release rod — Release — Clutch — Torque — Clutch centre — Driven gear — Clutch housing

How the piston and crank connect with the clutch via the primary drive.

Every powered two-wheeler needs the four main transmission elements to move forward, although these vary in type and detail from bike to bike. There's a further main subdivision of transmission types—manual and automatic. Manual transmission is the most common system for motorcycles, although some bike manufacturers, most notably Guzzi and Honda, have played around with automatic transmission in the past. Automatic transmission is the standard for mopeds and scooters, although some of these sport manual systems.

Primary drive

This is the link between the crankshaft—spinning merrily around propelled by the connecting rods and pistons—and the clutch. The connection is usually achieved either by chain or belt, or more commonly these days, gear. To propel machine and rider forward, especially from a standstill and at low engine speeds, we need plenty of torque—the twisting force that ultimately manifests itself at the back wheel.

The primary drive is the first stage in generating sufficient torque to get the bike moving. A typical arrangement is a smaller gear (the input or drive gear) on the end of the crank driving (by gear, chain, or belt) a larger gear (the driven or output gear) around the clutch housing. The ratios of these gears dictate by how much the torque at the crank is multiplied. If the input gear has half the number of teeth of the output gear, the output gear turns at half the speed and doubles the torque of the input gear. If the output has three times the teeth, it turns at a third of the speed of the input and produces three times the torque, and so on.

The process of torque multiplication and reduction continues throughout the drive train to deliver the optimum amount of torque for what the rider wants the bike to do.

Clutch

The clutch's job is to disconnect the running engine from the gearbox and final drive. If it wasn't there, the engine would have to be stopped every time the bike stopped. It also allows drive to be disengaged so you can change gears without crashing through the gearbox and stressing the components. In order to do this smoothly, it has to work progressively via the rider's input to the handlebar lever.

There are different types of clutch around, but they all have one thing in common—they work through friction.

Most manual clutches found on bikes these days consist of a drum or outer driven by the primary, as described above, mounted on the gearbox's input shaft. This is free to turn independently of the input shaft when the clutch is disengaged. The clutch center is splined to the input shaft. When it turns, the gearbox turns. The drum and the center are linked by a number of plates, plain steel and friction, which again are steel, but also have inserts of friction material.

The friction plates have teeth on their outer diameter that locate in the drum, and the plain ones have teeth that locate with the clutch center. The clutch pressure plate pulls the lot together using the clutch springs, and the friction between the sets of plates lets the engine drive the gearbox. When the clutch lever is pulled in, the pressure plate is moved slightly away from the plates, which means there is insufficient friction for the engine to drive the gearbox.

Wet multi-plate clutches are the most common setup. "Wet" means the plates run in oil to keep

BMW's F650 shows the crank, primary drive, gearbox interface, although the belt final drive is unusual.

Clutch drum *driven by primary gears.*

Clutch center *connects to gearbox.*

Clutch plates *alternating plain and friction plates. Friction plates spin with the engine, so when pressed against plain plates, spin the gearbox.*

Pressure plate *applies and releases pressure on friction plates.*

them cool and "multi-plate" means there is more than one set of plates. The use of numerous plates allows the diameter of the clutch to be kept small, but there is still a sufficient area of friction material to handle the torque generated without clutch slip

Some designs use single or double-plate clutches—for example, BMW Boxers and Guzzis where the crankshaft is in line with the frame, the clutch mounted on the end of the crank and running at engine speed. These plates are larger in diameter and have to run dry to deal with the torque. As they run at engine speed, torque multiplication takes place elsewhere in the drive train.

Smaller bikes, such as mopeds and scooters, that have automatic transmission run a different type of clutch. Some are governed by centrifugal force: as the revs rise, shoes like those in a brake drum are thrust into contact with a clutch outer, taking up drive. The other type is called ball and ramp: as engine speed rises and the clutch outer rotates faster, ball bearings acting on angled ramps against the pressure plate rise on the ramps to engage drive. This type of clutch is very similar to the wet multi-plate units found on bigger bikes.

Manual clutch operation can be by cable or hydraulic. Hydraulic systems are usually found only on high-end sport machines. They provide a lighter action than cable, for the same reasons that hydraulic brakes have more feel and force than cable systems.

Gearbox

The gearbox's job is as simple as its parts look complex. It's there to make the engine turn at a reasonable speed whatever the desired road speed. A side effect of this is that it dictates the number of power strokes needed during each revolution of the rear wheel, as dictated by the need to accelerate machine and rider from rest or low speed.

As internal combustion engine makes usable power in only very narrow power bands; gearboxes containing the correct ratios are required to make the most of what is there and keep the power band as wide as possible. Let's say you're on a sportbike, accelerating hard in second towards 10,000rpm. Clearly you wouldn't want the rear wheel spinning at the same rate as the engine—you'd almost be clear for takeoff. Instead, you want the right amount of torque, as set by the manufacturer getting its torque multiplication sums right, to provide linear acceleration until it's time for the next gearshift. If the ratios are right

Input shaft

6th 2nd 4th 3rd 5th 1st

Final drive sprocket

2nd 6th 4th 3rd 5th 1st

Output shaft

Clutch

Here's how it all hangs together in a typical constant mesh, six-speed motorcycle gearbox.

(and they should be if the manufacturer has been attentive), the rev counter drops to the bottom of the power band when you change gear. Then it rises again as you open the throttle, until you run out of gears, power and, ultimately, road.

Ratios on road bikes are chosen for flexibility rather than outright performance. By contrast, race bike ratios are chosen to work in extremely narrow power bands at the top of the rev range. Hence, first gear on a race bike makes it hard to pull away from the lights without slipping the clutch—but then race bikes only have to pull away from standstill once per outing, where a road bike has to do it many times. That's why it's equipped with higher ratios (lower gears) at the bottom of the 'box.

Gearboxes contain a number of gear pairs, usually between four and six. The principles of torque multiplication apply here too, first gear being a small cog on the input shaft driving a much larger one on the output shaft. At the other end of the scale, top gear consists of a gear on the input shaft that is the same size or sometimes larger than the one on the output. This ensures that there's plenty of thrust in the lower gears for acceleration, yet comfortable cruising in the higher ones with, power permitting, enough oomph for overtaking and so on. Usually gears are in constant mesh, whether they

are driving or being driven or not, and slide and engage on their respective shafts as they're selected by the gear shift, which moves the relevant pair of gears together on the shafts.

Final drive

The most common final drive system in current use is chain and sprockets, a small front and larger rear linked by a roller chain. There's also the less common belt type, as found on Harley-Davidsons, for example. As the section on chain care explains, the conventional chain and sprocket arrangement is very susceptible to road dirt and the elements, so regular maintenance is essential to slow the rate of the inevitable wear of both chain and sprockets.

Some bikes use shaft-drive systems. These are relatively low-maintenance and have better longevity than chains and sprockets, but are heavy, adding to unsprung weight, and don't transfer power as efficiently as chains. It's also much harder to change final drive ratios, should you wish to. What's more, there's the problem of torque reaction on a trailing throttle or under hard acceleration as the system struggles to deal with its own backlash between the gear teeth or the sudden take up of drive. And as chains and sprockets are cheaper to manufacture than shafts, it's likely that manufacturers will stick with those for the foreseeable future.

A BMW F650's final belt drive. Is this the way forward, or have rumors of the chain's demise been greatly exaggerated?

Tuning four-strokes

Tuning engines can mean many different things. In some ways, a service is a form of tuning because you adjust components to their optimum settings and replace parts as required. You're effectively tuning the engine to behave as it did when it was new. To most people, though, tuning is about more performance. They want their bike to go faster, and for that the engine needs to make more power and torque.

Engines basically convert the chemical energy in gas into usable power and torque. So it makes sense that the more gas an engine can burn, the more power and torque you can get out of it. This is true to a point, but you can't just shove in more fuel, because there won't be enough air to burn it properly unless that side of the induction process is addressed. And even if there is sufficient air, the engine may not make more power if it burns inefficiently, or loses the extra power through friction.

An inlet tract and valve. This is where it all begins, and things have to be right here for your engine to make optimum power.

So tuning can almost be summed up as burning more fuel, extracting energy more completely, and losing less of whatever the motor produces. First, look at what's stopping the engine getting that air and fuel in, and make them more efficient. For getting air/fuel into and out of the engine, this means looking at the air box and filters, carbs or throttle bodies, inlet and exhaust tracts in the cylinder head, valves, camshafts, and exhaust system.

Don't charge straight in and cut bits out of the cylinder head hoping to improve flow. Modern computer-designed cylinder heads are exceedingly good already, and it's easier to make them worse rather than better. Most people start by replacing the standard air filter since this is generally quite restrictive. By fitting a filter that can flow air more easily, you've already reduced one of the restrictions—and you've done it without great expense. You also risk making the mixture dangerously lean unless the issue of fuel supply is also addressed.

As the cylinder head is one of the biggest factors controlling how well an engine can breathe, it makes sense to tune it. But this should really be left to professionals, who have the experience to know what works and why. Most amateurs will dive in, make all the ports larger and change the shape to something they think looks nice. But when they run the engine it has less power. Bigger isn't always best, and once you've ground metal out it's hard to put it back in again.

Perhaps one of the most effective forms of tuning for road bikes is blueprinting. The motivation of blueprinting an engine isn't just to get more performance, although that is invariably a byproduct of it. Blueprinting is, as the name suggests, modifying an engine until it is exactly as the original designer's blueprint intended, before the accountants and processes that rule mass-production took over.

Although mass-production means we get our bikes cheaper, it also means there are power-sapping production tolerances to be met. The first bike off the production line might be just right, but 500 bikes later

the bits in the milling machines will be worn. Of course they're replaced as required but manufacturers still build to tolerances, which means you might get one bike exactly right but another where those key machine tools were at the limit.

We see the results of this most often on the dyno. It's possible to test two bikes of the same age, make, and model but see different results (as much as 15–20 percent) and most of this is due to production tolerances.

When an engine is blueprinted it's stripped down to the individual components and each is measured and weighed to make sure it matches the others. Pistons, for example, will be machined so they all weigh the same, eliminating strain on the crank and con-rods, reducing vibration and giving smoother power delivery. They will also be machined to give the same amount of valve-to-piston clearance in all the cylinders.

This principle is applied throughout the engine until you end up with a perfect engine. It generally makes more power because the tolerances are correct, should be more reliable because it's only tuned to its design spec, and is certainly nicer to use.

The next step usually involves component lightening, polishing, and other practices of the tuner's esoteric art.

A two-stroke may have fewer moving parts, in that there are no valves and camshafts to worry about, but blueprinting works here too. The main concern is still how the mixture gets in and out of the engine, and how quickly.

Tuning can become extreme, however. And the more power you have, the harder—and more expensive—it becomes to get even more. There will also come a point when your engine becomes so focused it's not very practical or pleasant to ride on the road. It might only make useable power at the top of the rev range and that's no good for road riding. A broad spread through the rev range is best for street bikes. For this reason, it's important to know what you want to achieve through tuning, and why, before you start.

Carburetors

Gas ignites and burns easily, but getting it to do this inside an engine isn't as simple as it first seems. For complete and efficient combustion, air and fuel need to be mixed in the right proportions. This is usually 12:1 to 13:1, which means 12 to 13 pounds of air for each pound of gas.

The fuel-to-air ratio can change dramatically depending on what an engine is being asked to do. For instance, starting a cold engine might require a mixture as rich as 4 to 5:1.

That sounds incredibly rich, but bear in mind that this isn't the ratio achieved in the cylinder. Because the engine is starting, the fuel isn't atomized as well as it might be and the low air speed struggles to carry the fuel efficiently. So even before it reaches the cylinder, some of the fuel has dropped out of suspension—effectively making the mixture leaner.

The idea is to end up with a richer than normal mix in the cylinder because a rich mixture is easier to ignite—and that makes starting easier. In contrast, a cruising ratio might be as lean as 18:1.

So much for mixture proportions, but how does a carburetor actually work? Carbs work because they have something called a venturi. This is essentially a restriction where the passage through the carburetor narrows, then opens up again. As air passes through the venturi it drops in pressure, and it is this differential that can be utilized.

Fuel from your tank flows into the carbs and is held in the float-bowl, where it waits until something causes it to do otherwise. In this case, the otherwise is low pressure in the venturi, which is connected to the float-bowl by a passage. Although it's only at atmospheric pressure, the air in the float-bowl is relatively high compared to the venturi. This drives fuel up the passage, through the main jet into an emulsion tube and finally into the air stream, where it is broken down into tiny droplets that are carried into the combustion chamber by the air.

The most common type of carburetor fitted to bikes is the CV (constant velocity) carb. This is a clever device that controls the flow of air through the venturi to help deliver the correct amount of fuel, regardless of how open or shut the throttle plate is, by maintaining the correct pressure in the venturi.

In effect, the rider doesn't directly control the slide in the carb. Instead, the carb monitors the vacuum in the inlet tract, which is controlled by the rider using the throttle plate, and uses this to operate a vacuum slide. The greater the vacuum the more the slide lifts. It sounds complicated but isn't really. It's just a system to help stop the engine from bogging down.

A slide, or flat-slide, carb works in the same way, but the throttle directly opens and closes the slide in the venturi. In effect you control the velocity of air, and therefore fuel.

It's possible to get more power using a flat-slide carb because there is less clutter in the inlet tract when the throttle is wide open. But the drawback is that the rider must have a good understanding of what the engine requires and the necessary skill to operate the throttle accordingly.

You can't just open the throttle with a flat-slide carb to accelerate—especially from low to mid-revs. Because the engine isn't revving very fast, the velocity of air through the carb is relatively slow. Suddenly opening the slide effectively increases the diameter of the venturi, reducing its effectiveness, and also lowers the vacuum in the inlet tract.

This means there isn't enough pressure differential to move enough fuel through the carb and not enough velocity to carry it efficiently to the cylinder. The engine will become starved of fuel and bog. In some cases the engine will recover, but if the revs continue to drop and the throttle remains wide open, the revs fall and the problem gets worse.

CV carbs let the engine run far more smoothly than slide carbs because they avoid this. And they also allow you to ride the bike without worrying about the throttle and fueling demands of the engine.

A typical bank of CV carbs from an inline four.

Constant velocity (CV) carburetor
Air is routed up into the vacuum chamber via a hole in the base of the piston.

Air at atmospheric pressure fills the area below the diaphragm.

Return spring helps to stabilize the piston.

Throttle as the throttle is opened, low pressure is created in the vacuum chamber and the piston begins to rise.

Needle the piston has a tapered needle attached that blocks the fuel flow. As it is lifted, gas is drawn up by the low pressure.

Slide Carburetor
Piston is directly controlled by the twist grip.

Air pressure drops as the piston is lifted and more air flows.

Needle the piston has a tapered needle attached that blocks the fuel flow. As it is lifted gas is drawn up by the low pressure.

Carburetor **tuning**

Tuning carburetors and actually improving their performance is a true black art, especially as they have been around for so long and most things have been tried already. So the first thing to consider is what exactly you are trying to do.

There are many reasons to fiddle with a carburetor. It might be to get rid of that annoying flat-spot at 5,000rpm or to make the engine run smoother. Or you may have fitted a new exhaust with different flow characteristics. Whatever it is, chances are it'll be more complicated than you think.

However, there are a few things you can do. The most common alteration to carbs is to balance or synchronize them, assuming there is more than one carb, that is. Balancing the carbs ensures they are all drawing the same amount of air and fuel—so you get the same performance and response from each cylinder. Once adjusted correctly, the power delivery will definitely feel smoother. Unbalanced carbs can even lead to a degree of vibration that feels like serious engine problems.

Balancing is done by connecting vacuum gauges to the inlet tracts and adjusting the synchronization screws on the carbs. This a very fine way of adjusting the throttle plate so the vacuum in the inlet tracts are the same. Ideally, the vacuum levels of the carbs will match, although sometimes carbs are balanced as pairs, with the inner and outer pairs on a four-cylinder machine running differently. Check your manual if unsure.

It's also important to keep carbs clean—both internally and externally. Dirt tends to accumulate on carbs because of the residue that invariably forms on them. In time, this greasy paste can cause problems and certainly doesn't make it easy to work on or even check the condition of carbs. Careful use of a degreaser is normally enough to keep them clean.

Cleaning carbs internally needs to be done rarely, but if a bike has been stored with fuel in the carbs, it can evaporate from the system and leave a gummy residue, which blocks jets. In this case, the carb should be stripped and cleaned or at least have some aerosol carb cleaner run through it.

It's not so common now, but people used to scrap their existing carbs in favor of ones with bigger throats. The logic is that if more mixture can get into the engine, it'll make more power. While there is a hint of truth about this, it isn't that simple.

As we mentioned previously, carbs mix fuel relative to the vacuum in their venturi. As you get a lower pressure with a smaller venturi, so the reverse is true. Although you increase the flow potential of the engine by fitting bigger carbs, what you normally get is awful fueling because they're unable thoroughly to mix the correct amount of fuel.

In some ways, a smaller bore carburetor is better for road use because it will improve the mid-range response of the engine. Manufacturers often use this trick when they make less extreme versions of their bikes. Yamaha did this when it fitted the R1 engine into the FZ-1.

To set a carb up properly, it's wise to measure the air/fuel ratio in the exhaust. Most dyno houses have this equipment and can run the bike to check that the mixture isn't too rich or lean. To affect the overall ratio of the bike it's necessary to change the main jet. The bigger the hole in it, the greater the flow of fuel and so the richer the mixture becomes.

There are other adjustments too. In most cases, it's possible to 'lift the needle.' This simply means adjusting the height of the needle relative to the slide. Most adjustable needles have three or four grooves at the top, and by moving a clip to different grooves you can raise or lower the needle. This has the effect of allowing more or less fuel to flow through the needle jet for a given throttle opening.

Adjustable needle
The locating circlip can be raised or lowered on the needle to provide fine tuning.

Flat-Slide Carburetor
Mikuni TDMR40, supplied with the Suzuki GSX-R750W race kit. Note angled float bowl and offset main jet, designed to keep the carburetor compact and let it operate at a steep downdraft angle. (Suzuki)

Fuel **injection** systems

Despite carburetors being refined over many years to a point where they're taken for granted, the world moves on—and in the direction of fuel injection. Fuel injection is not a new technology. In fact, it's been around in cars for so long even the most basic models have it. In bikes, it isn't so common yet and usually only the premier bikes in each class are injected. But having said that, it's come and gone on bikes for the past couple of decades. Until recently, the most common excuse from the manufacturers has been that bikes rev across too broad a range to make efficient fuel injection systems. However, all of that is changing fast.

Honda injection system from the RC45. More and more sportbikes feature injection.

Fuel Injector

Fuel filter

Solenoid coil

Plunger

Seat

Needle valve

Pintle

A fuel injection system is essentially made up of one or more injectors, a number of sensors, and a control unit. Unlike carburetors, which are governed by the laws of physics and therefore know what to do intrinsically, a fuel injection system has to be told. For this reason, a fuel-injected bike is covered in sensors.

You might think a cylinder with a displacement of 250cc will suck in a quarter of a liter of air with each induction stroke, but this is not quite the case. Even with the throttle wide open, most engines only fill their cylinders between 80 and 95 percent of their maximum capacity because there's so little time to do it and so many restrictions. The point at which an engine most effectively fills its cylinders will be when peak torque occurs.

Because the engine doesn't always draw in the same amount of air, the most important thing the ECU (electronic control unit) needs to know is how fast the engine is revving and how far open the throttle is. Using this information, and knowing roughly how well the engine will fill its cylinder under those conditions, it sets off to a library stored in its memory to find out how much fuel to inject.

Unfortunately, that is not enough. If the engine is being started cold, it needs a rich mixture, so engine temperature needs checking. The system also needs to know the air pressure—higher pressure means denser air, and that requires more fuel to get the correct ratio. Remember, the ratio is by weight, not volume.

As if working out the correct amount of fuel to inject wasn't hard enough, the ECU also has to deliver precisely that amount—and this can be a job in itself. When you turn the key on an injected bike, you'll hear a fuel pump whirr into life. This pumps fuel into a rail connected to the injectors, effectively making them little faucets. When an injector opens, fuel flows from the rail into the engine.

The amount of fuel flowing depends on three things: the flow rate of the injector; the amount of time it's open; and the flow rate from the pump. The injector's rating remains the same but the open time and pressure both vary, and these need to be taken into account too.

The list of information required by the ECU goes on, and the more there is, the better the end result will be. Armed with all the information, the ECU determines how long it needs to open each injector to deliver the required fuel. It then sends a timed signal to the injector, which opens and closes a small nozzle in its end. The opening time is a matter of milliseconds.

This is where injectors better carbs, though. By forcing fuel through a nozzle under pressure, the fuel is equally atomized in all conditions. And the smaller the fuel droplets are, the better they can mix with the air. End result: more efficiency and power.

For maximum performance, some bikes have more than one injector per cylinder. The extra injector is normally fitted at the mouth of the inlet tract and only kicks in at high revs. One advantage of this system is that the injected fuel is more evenly spread through the inlet charge, which gives a better burn and more performance.

A single injector, capable of supplying enough fuel at high revs, would only have to open very briefly at lower revs, concentrating the fuel in a portion of the intake air. An injector with a smaller capacity would have to stay open longer to deliver the same amount of fuel, and in that time more air would pass by it.

Electronics also bring a greater degree of control. Most bikes reference different fuel maps depending on what gear they're in. Fuel injection allows manufacturers to control things down to the very last detail, and that means bikes can respond better, whatever our needs.

Inside an injector. The actual engineering looks simple, but injection requires complex electronics to control it effectively.

Exhaust systems

Exhaust systems aren't just there to keep the noise down. In fact, the only reason engines have silencers fitted at all is because legislation says they must—being quiet doesn't improve performance.... But even without this legislation, bikes would still have exhaust pipes of some sort because they are just as responsible for engine performance as any other part.

Yamaha exhaust system features that company's famous EXUP valve that helps optimize power delivery.

Cables

Servomotor

Power valve

Modern exhaust systems are built from a number of materials. Low-performance or economy bikes still tend towards steel exhaust systems because they're cheap and functional. High-performance bikes use more exotic lightweight materials, such as titanium and carbon fiber. This has little to no effect on engine power but a large impact on your wallet. They're actually more about saving weight than anything else.

The design of modern sportbike exhausts has come a long way since the late 1990s, and a lot of work goes into them. For starters, they have to be the right bore. In many ways, you'd think a bigger bore pipe would be best because it can flow more gas, but this isn't always the case.

A big-bore pipe helps an engine make good top-end power because it can flow large amounts of gas quickly. However, a smaller bore pipe can give a useful boost to low- and mid-range power by keeping the gas velocity up, which helps it to pull burned gas from the cylinder.

As well as gas flow, pressure waves can be used in exhaust systems, and are absolutely crucial in two-strokes. These pulses are caused by the flow of gas and by the valves opening and closing. When the exhaust valve closes, it sends a high-pressure wave down the exhaust pipe and part of the energy in the wave will be reflected as a negative wave back down the pipe when it reaches the end. Timed correctly, this negative wave will arrive just as the valve opens and encourage the gas in the cylinder to start moving. This effect only works at certain points in the rev range.

The formation of the pipes has an effect on power too. Some four-cylinder bikes have a 4-2-1, where the four header pipes converge into two pairs, before converging again into a single pipe. Others have a 4-1. There are advantages to each. A 4-2-1 system promotes mid-range power but isn't as efficient at high revs. The 4-1 system is the opposite, boosting top end but sacrificing some mid-range.

Power valves are also fairly common. They can be found in the ports of two-stroke motors and in the exhausts of four-strokes. In each case, they fool the engine into thinking that it has the best of both worlds. They do this by altering the exhaust port timing, the tuned length of the exhaust pipe or the configuration. Either way, the idea is to use the exhaust gas to help get more gas out of the cylinder and so more fresh mixture in.

Two-strokes are perhaps more responsive to the effects of exhaust pipes. You only have to look at their swoopy shapes and bulges to see that a lot of thought goes into them. In general, they aim to return a low-pressure wave at the exhaust port as it opens and a high-pressure wave just before it shuts. This makes a big difference to the scavenging ability of the engine, and can enhance and move the power band.

Two-stroke expansion chamber exhaust system
Spent gases rush out as a high-pressure wave, gradually expanding and losing velocity until reaching the reversed cone. Gases are compressed by the reverse cone and a proportion returns as a reverse pulse. This creates high pressure at the exhaust port, stopping fresh mixture escaping down the exhaust.

Four-stroke exhaust
System of internal baffles keeps noise down, hopefully not sacrificing too much power.

Race & performance exhausts

We've already looked at standard exhaust systems and seen that reducing noise isn't really what they are there for. So when tuning bikes, it makes sense to get rid of the noise restrictions, as these normally work by forcing the exhaust gas back and forth through a series of noise-deadening chambers—and that's quite restrictive.

Yoshimura race can
There are dozens of can manufacturers, Yoshimura is one of the older established companies.

Harris carbon can
Carbon fiber is a popular material for exhaust cans. And extremely fashionable too.

Yoshimura Tri-oval
Another offering from the celebrated tuning firm. Slimline form gives plenty of ground clearance.

Bike exhaust systems are not made in one piece, which allows just the silencer to be replaced without touching the rest of the system. This is a quick and simple modification, and it's quite cheap too. The standard silencers are normally replaced with slip-on race cans. The slip-on refers to their ease of fitment and the race bit simply means they're not road legal.

In almost all cases, the exhaust gas is free to travel straight through the center of the can because it does away with the sound chambers. The can is lined with a perforated tube and sound-deadening material, though, so it does cut down noise a little bit. Over time, its ability to do this will reduce and eventually it'll need repacking.

By increasing the ability of gas to flow through the exhaust system, it can move faster and in larger amounts. As far as the engine is concerned, this means it can rev more easily because it does not have to push gas through the exhaust system. But there are other implications.

With less pressure in the exhaust, it's easier for burned gases in the combustion chamber to get out. And the faster that happens, the quicker fresh mixture can be drawn in to replace it. The result is more power, although it's wise to check the bike's fuel on a hilly road, because fitting an end-can might cause the engine to run lean.

One tradeoff might be a slight loss of mid-range power. As new mixture is drawn into the combustion chamber, it can get sucked straight out of the exhaust port.

Race cans flow more gas, so the fuel system must also supply more fuel to keep the correct mixture. This is only a serious problem if the mixture becomes dangerously lean and happens to do so in the type of conditions in which you often ride—say, 7,000rpm with part-throttle. Having the bike set up on a dyno will reveal any potential problems and also allow the fueling to be optimized.

As well as replacing the end-can, people often replace the rest of the exhaust system. In the past, they did this because standard systems were built to a price and to give good results over a broad rev-range. By fitting aftermarket systems, people could pay for performance boosting features that increased engine performance in one area— usually top-end power for racing.

Now, though, many standard high-performance systems already come with features such as tapered header and crossover pipes. Both these features are designed to make best use of pressure waves and pulses traveling backwards and forwards through the exhaust. As with two-stroke exhausts, they're timed to reflect low-pressure waves on to the back of the exhaust valves just before they open, encouraging flow. A well-designed full-system can increase power by 3–10bhp.

Although it's always nice to increase the performance of your bike, there can be drawbacks. Some systems and even end-cans mean you have to remove a center stand. If this is something you use all the time, it's worth searching around to find a system that lets you retain this.

It is also worth remembering that most race cans and full-systems aren't street legal. So as well as being louder and drawing more attention to yourself, you might end up in trouble with the law.

It should be possible to fit a full system and end-can yourself with only a few tools. Generally, the system will fix to the exhaust ports with two Allen bolts per cylinder, have a couple of brackets under the engine, and finally be supported by a bracket or clamp on the end-can. It's important to get a good seal on any joints since gas leaks will reduce performance slightly, but more annoyingly, cause the bike to back fire on a shut throttle. Use an exhaust joint sealer and check for leaks' once fitted.

Section through ignition map

Load

Signal from load sensor

Advance

25°   30°   35°

Programmed information stored in computer memory

Engine speed

Signal from engine speed sensor

Electronic **C**ontrol **U**nits & **ignition**

The majority of bikes now have a small black box tucked away somewhere under the plastics—it's the ECU (electronic control unit). These seemingly impregnable boxes control most of the things going on in the engine. But that may not be as much as you think. At most, an ECU governs the fuel injection, ignition timing, and sometimes a power valve or two.

Dynojet Power Commander

This clever device allows the info going to and from the ECU to be manipulated to optimize fueling and/or ignition.

Schematic of a typical modern motorcycle system. At its heart lies the electronic control unit that collects information from sensors all over the bike then tells the key components what to do.

So why have them? Because they're more versatile and accurate than mechanical systems, that's why. They're also smaller, lighter, and cheaper to produce.

Fuel injection is perhaps the biggest user of black boxes. We've already touched on carburetors and what a good job they do, despite the many conditions they have to work under. Fuel injection, on the other hand, is essentially dumb and has to be told what to do under each condition it might encounter. For this reason, it needs good, up-to-date information before it makes any decision.

The black box collects information from a number of sensors on the bike. These include throttle position, engine revs, crankshaft position, water temperature, air temperature, and air pressure. Generally, more sensors mean the ECU can make a more accurate decision on how much fuel to inject. It then sends a signal to open and close the injector long enough to deliver that precise amount of fuel.

ECUs also control ignition timing. Again, to make the best decision possible, they need information. So at any time, the ECU will know what position the crankshaft is in and what demands are being made of the engine. It then references that information against a table stored in its memory and advances or retards the ignition as required.

In many ways, it's easier to tune bikes using the ECU than it is to do the same job manually. There are several devices available, such as Dynojet's Power Commander and Yoshimura's EMS, which plug into

H32577

**Four-stroke,
four-valve cylinder**

*A dramatic presentation of
what happens inside a four-
strode bike's cylinders.*

the bike's ECU and alter the signals. Doing this allows you to manipulate the information being sent to, or from, the ECU. So you can control the fueling and ignition at almost any point in the rev range without affecting anything else—something that's difficult to do with carbs or mechanical ignitions. To set it up, you just need someone with a dyno, load cell and the necessary software and experience.

The potential to exploit black-box technology is very exciting. Already we've seen how Suzuki used it to good effect with its dual throttle-valve injector bodies. The result is a virtual CV carb with injectors.

In the past, fuel-injected bikes suffered in similar ways to flat-slide carbs (although to a lesser degree because of the injectors), because the rider had direct control over the throttle plate. With its GSX-R series, Suzuki has incorporated a second throttle valve controlled by the black box to maintain the optimum intake velocity—a helping hand on the throttle, if you like.

In theory, the same unit could also control variable length inlet tracts to boost mid-range and top-end power. Honda has already fitted traction control to some of its bikes, but there's no reason

why this couldn't be extended to sporty models too. And, with the correct sensors, you could even end up with a bike that knows when it's raining and switches to a softer fuel injection map for more controllable delivery as well as turning on the traction control system.

Ignition

The ignition is the system responsible for igniting the air/fuel mixture in the combustion chamber. This is more difficult than it first sounds, though. For starters, the mixture has to be ignited at just the right time to give maximum power, and in engines this is measured in degrees of crank rotation before or after the piston is at top dead center (TDC), or highest point.

It surprises many people to know that, in many cases, the air/fuel mixture is actually lit before the piston reaches the top of its stroke. They know that when the mixture burns it expands and pushes down on the piston, but what they forget is that the mixture burns—it doesn't explode.

For this reason, the inertia of the crank is enough for it to keep turning, despite the burn starting while it is coming up the bore. The idea behind starting the burn early is simple. It takes time for the mixture to burn and increase the cylinder pressure.

Sadly, time is something the engine doesn't have (at high revs there are only a few hundredths of a second for the mixture to burn), so by starting the burn early, the burn is more developed as the piston starts on its down-stroke, which is where we want maximum pressure.

It's also worth bearing in mind that as the piston travels down the bore, it increases the volume of the cylinder and reduces the pressure, weakening the effect of combustion. In fact, most of the useful work done by the burned gas happens in the early stages of the stroke. Ignition is timed to give maximum efficiency on the power stroke.

The burn is started by the spark plug. By jumping a high voltage across a gap, a spark is produced. This excites the molecules adjacent to the spark sufficiently to start the combustion process. From there, the flame spreads out through the mixture, in much the same way as a ripple on a pond, until all the mixture is burned or something causes it to stop.

There are several things capable of stopping the burn. Over the past few pages, we've mentioned the importance of a good even mixture several times. If the mixture is uneven, this can stop the burn. Think of it like a forest fire.

In ideal conditions, the fire will spread from tree to tree and burn the whole forest. But if the trees are too spread out (that is, they're too lean) the fire won't be able to jump the gap and there will be areas of unburned trees. This is what happens if there are excessively lean areas in the mixture. There are also small areas around the cylinder walls that don't burn properly because the heat energy for exciting the molecules is absorbed by the metal.

Compression ratios play a role too, and you'll normally find they are increased when an engine is tuned. By compressing the mixture, you're cramming the air and fuel molecules closer together, which makes it easy for each molecule to ignite the next. It's the same as our forest trees when they're planted very close together.

So the conditions have to be right for the mixture to burn. But if the ignition system doesn't deliver enough voltage, or there's a bad connection, the spark may not be strong enough to ignite the mixture properly or even jump the gap at all. If that happens, there will be only a partial burn or possibly no burn at all—a misfire. For this reason, it's important to keep the ignition system in good order.

It's also harder for the ignition to light a lean mixture or one under high compression. In both cases, a stronger spark is required, something that old ignitions sometimes struggled to supply. This is why there used to be lots of aftermarket ignitions for sale. It's not so much of a problem now, because bikes that need it have high-energy ignitions capable of igniting the mixture under normal conditions, and even after the engine has been tuned. They also reduce the frequency of partial burns or misfires.

Ignition reduced to its basics

At the pickup the crank tells the CDI (a basic ECU) where it's at in its stroke. Knowing this, the CDI tells which coil to fire and when. Each pair of coils on a four-cylinder fires both its two plugs simultaneously—the so-called wasted spark, where one plug has no fresh mixture to ignite. The advantage of the system in this case is that only two coils are needed for a four-cylinder bike.

Main wiring harness

Pickup unit

Ignition coil

Ignition coil

CDI unit

Spark plug

Spark plug

Frame
types

So what does your frame do? At its most basic, it keeps your backside off the ground, your wheels apart from each other, and provides a place for your engine to live. But there is much more to a frame than that.

Looking beyond the fundamentals, it holds the swingarm and forks at the right heights, angles, and distances to optimize handling. It must also be rigid enough to keep the wheels in line under the considerable forces of braking, acceleration, and cornering. Sufficient rigidity is needed to maintain the steering head's vertical relationship to the machine and swingarm pivot's horizontal relationship regardless of the forces of turning, stopping, and accelerating. The design and construction of the frame also has a role to play in insulating the rest of the machine and the rider from damaging and irritating engine vibrations.

A machine's center of gravity is critical to how it behaves under acceleration, braking, and cornering, so the frame is designed with this in mind. As you accelerate, maximum traction through the back tire is desirable. When you brake, you want traction to be optimized at the front. When cornering, it's best if both tires grip by the same amount and the bike turns in easily. Generally, these are all improved if the center of gravity is high, but too high and there can be too much weight transfer, meaning wheelies and stoppies everywhere. If the center of gravity is lower, the bike will be easier to steer, although more lean is required to make a given turn and there's less traction than with a high center of gravity. To provide the best of all worlds, some compromise is required in how the bike's key components are positioned.

When is an **engine** a **frame?**

Some bikes barely have a frame at all, using the engine as a so-called "stressed member" from which the front and rear ends are hung. In these cases, the engine is effectively the frame. One of the simplest examples to illustrate the concept is the Honda "semi-pivotless" system (as on the 900RR), where the swingarm pivots around a mount at the back of the gearbox casting. Obviously that bike has a frame, as we understand them conventionally, for the front end and engine, so let's take another example of a "proper" stressed member design. BMW's recent Boxers have the front as well as the rear suspension attached to the engine, with subframes carrying the rest of the bike's components.

Cradle frames

These are a very conventional design and have been around for years. The engine is bolted in a "cradle" formed by the bottom tubes, and the head is bolted to the top rail or rails. For greater rigidity, there may be a pair of down tubes too, and larger more powerful cradle-framed bikes tend to adopt this design. The most popular material for cradle frames is steel tubing, although box-section steel is sometimes used.

Beam frames

The twin-spar, "perimeter" or beam frame is very widely used, especially on sportbikes. Typically two large beams join the headstock to the swingarm pivot although, as mentioned before, some bikes' swingarms pivot off the back of the gearbox. Extruded or box-section aluminum are the most common materials used in these designs, with alloy castings for the swingarm pivot, although some still use steel for the whole construction. The frame wraps around the top sides of the engine to make the motor a partially stressed member, its casings being beefed up to improve load-bearing. Some beam frames also feature lower steel rails, which form an additional cradle for the engine.

Spine frames

These are popular on scooters and mopeds and are often made of pressed steel. Honda's 919 is an example of a larger bike that uses the concept. The 919 has a box section spine from which the engine hangs, while alloy castings provide the swingarm pivot points. Spine frames are well suited to automated mass-production techniques, which explains their appeal to manufacturers of budget machines.

Trellis frames

These usually use the engine as a stressed member. Straight pieces of round or square section material, usually steel, are welded together to form lightweight but very rigid frames. The most celebrated modern example of the trellis is from Ducati. Light, minimalist, but just enough to do the job. Looks gorgeous too.

Other frame stuff

Back in the 1970s and 1980s, when engine performance was rapidly eclipsing that of the chass[is], a huge frame aftermarket grew up. These days, mos[t] standard frames are more than adequate. But if you fancy or require the ultra-trick, there are still plenty o[f] companies out there that w[ill] build a bespoke frame. If you're unlucky enough to suffer a get-off, most frames—apart from the terminally twisted—can be[e] fixed. To check for proper true, the chassis will have [to] be analyzed by a specialist[,] which means a fairly extensive strip down. One easier way to check for damage is to look at whee[l] alignment (see your manual). Sometimes the damage can be seen in obvious folds and buckles [in] the frame. And if you're a wheelie monster, ham-fiste[d] set-downs might lead to o[val] bearing housings at the headstock. Steady now.

Front Suspension

he front forks are one of the
usiest components on any bike.
hey have to optimize the tire's
ontact with the road, both in a
raight line and while cornering.
hey must smooth the ride over
neven surfaces and minimize
ive under braking. Then they also
eed to give the rider adequate
eedback about what the front
nd's doing in any circumstance.
Quite a lot to be going on at once.

s far as the basic anatomy of motorcycle forks
es, stanchions (also known as sliders) travel up
nd down the fork leg. There are two basic types in
ommon use these days—right way up (RWU),
anchion above leg and upside down (USD),
anchion below leg. There are other systems, but
lescopic forks are by far the most common.

Rebound damping *While the springs will bounce back merrily on their own, the rebound damping uses oil/or sometimes gas forced through valves to slow the process.*

Preload *adjuster takes up sag in the front springs. Doesn't make the spring "harder," although it can feel that way.*

Compression damping *as with the rebound, uses oil and sometimes gas to slow the bike's progress down the fork's travel.*

Springs

Internal springs take care of the basic rates of dive and rebound. At their cheapest and most basic, springs have equally wound coils, which compress evenly. Because this simple type doesn't become stiffer as it compresses, there's a risk of the forks bottoming out when severe bumps are encountered at speed. Better than these are multi-rate springs, which can be two springs of different strengths, or single springs wound to different rates at either end. The softer spring takes care of smaller bumps and shocks, and, as it compresses completely, the second stronger spring or section of spring takes effect.

Best of all are "progressive" springs, where the distance between the spring's coils gets progressively less along the length of the spring. Progressive springs become stiffer as they compress and less stiff as they lengthen, the rate of which is optimized to account for the weight of the bike and that of a typical rider. The progressive nature of the springs means that small bumps are easily absorbed, and sudden larger bumps can be dealt with without the forks bottoming out.

Damping

When you hit a bump, the fork springs compress. The next thing they want to do is to extend, pushing the bike up—the energy they've just absorbed has to go somewhere. A series of bumps has the potential to tie suspension in knots, the bike bumping and jarring over the irregular surface.

Damping is the method of governing the rate at which the forks dive (compress) and spring back (rebound). Some mopeds, scooters, and lightweights get by with no damping at all or rely on friction.

Oil damping is used on other machines. Valves control the rate at which the oil passes on

compression and rebound. Gas and air have also been used to assist the damping.

Front suspension adjustment

Budget and smaller capacity bikes often have non-adjustable suspension, and for most riders of these machines, the absence of adjusters will go unnoticed. On larger bikes, particularly sportbikes and tourers, there are usually four main adjustable factors—preload, height of forks in the yokes, rebound damping, and compression damping.

Preload adjustment is found at the top of the forks and alters the effective length of the springs. It doesn't make the suspension softer or harder, but varies the ride height and the amount the bike "sags" on its suspension. Rebound adjusters are usually concentric with and internal to the preload adjusters and dictate the rate the forks extend after compression. At the bottom of the forks are the compression adjusters, which can be tweaked to control the rate of dive.

When your bike left the dealership when it was new, the suspension should have been set to the base setting suggested by the manufacturer in the owner's manual. These are invariably a best average, for average road conditions, riding style, and rider weight. But no road or rider conforms to an average, so feel free to fiddle with the adjusters. Just remember to do it gradually.

And unless you've bought the latest homologation race replica sportbike, your bike's suspension has been built down to a price. That's not to say it won't meet your needs—and lots of standard forks are excellent—but if you're a trackday demon or an ace on the roads, you might want something with more adjustment. Look at revalving the standard kit or replacing the springs. Or if you want to go all the way, buy some trick aftermarket forks.

Rear
suspension

Like the front forks, the rear shock (or shocks on a twin-shock bike) has plenty to do too. It has to optimize tire contact with the road in a straight line and in corners; smooth the ride over uneven surfaces; and give the rider feedback about what the tire's up to. Yet the rear suspension also has an important role in ensuring as much power as possible is delivered to the road without wheel spin or excessive compression and extension. If your bike had no rear suspension and any appreciable power, the back wheel would spend as much time off the road as it would in contact with it.

What's in a shock?

An external spring takes care of the basic rates of dive and rebound and, like the springs in the front forks, it is often "progressive" or "multi-rate," so it becomes stiffer as it compresses. As with the front suspension, progressive springs provide a more effective solution than multi-rate springs, which are just two springs of different rates.

On many monoshock bikes, a rising-rate linkage, connecting the shock to the swingarm and frame, means a cheaper-to-manufacture constant-rate spring can be used. All these methods prevent the travel being used up too quickly by severe bumps while making the spring compliant enough to deal with more moderate bumps.

That spring lives outside a damper unit, which is typically oil-filled to control the rates of shock compression and rebound. The oil passes through shim stacks (a bit like washers), which restrict the rate it can pass.

Shock adjustment

Cheap shocks, as found on budget bikes and many smaller machines, tend to rely on stiff springs and basic damping. More sophisticated shocks combine better multi-rate springs with adjustable damping for improved performance. Many use compressed gas to keep the oil under pressure, which prevents bubbles forming in it and damping being lost when the shock is working hard and fast. Apart from compression and rebound adjusters, some high-end shocks have additional high-speed damping adjusters to give the rear additional help when particularly violent bumps are encountered. Some have ride height adjusters too to raise the back of the bike and quicken steering.

Rear shock preload adjustment is usually by stepped collar or threaded rings on the shock body. Increasing it reduces sag and the bike sits a little higher. Remote preload adjusters are fitted to some shocks for ease of adjustment. Rebound adjustment is generally found at the bottom of the shock and compression at the top, sometimes on a remote adjuster.

Some shocks are non-adjustable, but it is often possible to fit springs of different rates and have the shock revalved or filled with a different grade of oil to change the way the unit behaves. There are plenty of specialists offering these services.

Most shocks on mass-produced bikes are built down to a budget, but as with front forks, many are excellent and more than adequate for all but racers and trackday nuts. Revalving and springs of different rates are the cheapest ways to tailor the standard equipment to your needs. There's a huge aftermarket out there for riders who simply want replacements and those who want extra performance, providing shocks that are often better and cheaper than original equipment.

The location of monoshocks in particular on a bike means they can get covered in road dirt and water flung off the back wheel. Fitting a hugger will protect the shock from the worst of this. They can run very hot as well because, apart from heat generated in the unit through its operation, it's also sited close to the engine and is away from the flow of cooling air. For that reason, damping systems have become progressively better over the years, especially in high-end shocks. Some keep the damping medium in a separate reservoir sited either remotely or on the back of the shock.

Compression damping Like on the front end oil damping slows the rate of dive. Gas is almost always involved on bigger bikes to help the oil hydraulics out.

Preload This particular shock lacks a remote preload adjuster, making C-wrench–induced skinned knuckles a near certainty.

Rebound damping This shock has a screw adjuster for rebound damping that slows the rate the shock extends at. Some others use knurled knobs.

Swingarms

Most swingarms supplied as standard on modern bikes are up to the job they're designed to do. Fundamentally they carry the back wheel, pivot off the back of the frame or engine, and are prevented from slamming the tire into the underside of the seat by the shocks or monoshock and its linkage.

Huge as they are, these alloy swingarms provide several times the rigidity of steel for proportionately less weight and allow plenty of bracing to be used for little mass tradeoff.

There's a lot more going on beyond the basic functions of a swingarm. As with frames, rigidity is an issue. In the old days, tubular swingarms on puny mounts allowed the wheel to flex sideways, which upset handling, but at that time the power of the bikes and their tires were such that there weren't too many demands on the (just about) adequate chassis of the era. Gusseting between the two forks of the swingarm and the pivot tube helped prevent flex. The usual material was tubular steel, but as power outputs rose and bikes got better, manufacturers started to use box section designs. The only problem was that the weight penalty started to increase as the section of these swingarms got bigger in line with further power hikes. Bracing got bigger and heavier too.

Modern swing

Today, things are different. Many bikes still use steel swingarms, but tubular ones are usually found only on twin-shock lightweights. Steel box section swingarms are still quite common too, particularly on middleweight budget standards.

Aluminum is the thing these days, particularly on high-performance bikes. Obviously it's lighter than steel but not as strong, although an alloy swingarm that's as strong and heavy as a steel arm is stiffer. So it's possible to build alloy swingarms that are just as stiff as steel but lighter. Alloy items are often internally and externally braced for more strength. This means the walls of the swingarm can be thinner and hence lighter.

Taking sides

Single-sided swingarms are a race-bred option designed for easy wheel changes in endurance competition. Hyper-rigid, but there's a weight penalty. Ducati top-end sportbikes have them (although the race bikes use magnesium or carbon while the less exotic street machines use alloy), but the Triumph 955i has gone back to a more

conventional system. Until recently Ducatis used a single-sider pivoting on the crankcase rather than the back of the gearbox or frame, as would be the usual practice, because of their long V-twin engines, which had to be mounted far back in the frame because of the cylinder sticking out the front. The Duke's wheelbase would have been too great for quick steering if it used a conventionally mounted swingarm that was long enough to accommodate wheel and shock.

Weight watchers

Swingarms play a big part in the complicated problem of unsprung weight—that's to say, those components that live below your bike's suspension, such as wheels, brakes, and swingarms. An amount of the suspension system's weight adds to the unsprung load too. Basically, the lower the proportion of unsprung weight to the sprung mass of the bike (the rest of it), the better the handling. The main reason for this is because unsprung mass gathers momentum on the move, upsetting the suspension. Therefore, a heavy bike on lighter running gear tends to be more composed than a pared-down sporter on the same chassis.

Swing out

So swingarms are a compromise between rigidity and weight. Many aftermarket options offer extra rigidity but not much of a weight advantage. A full works racing swingarm made from something exotic like magnesium or carbon fiber would offer the best of all worlds, but unless you're a full works rider, you probably won't feel any advantage.

There is a healthy aftermarket too, which first emerged in the old days of flexi-frames and swingarms. Often beautifully engineered with trick bracing, they can also offer the option of adjusting the wheelbase and revised linkages. Even these days, the bike manufacturers don't always get it exactly right, so there will always be alternatives.

Basic tubular steel swingarm, for a twin-shock (left) and alloy single-sider for a monoshock Ducati show both ends of the swingarm pendulum swing. Ducati has now made their race engines short enough to revert to a more conventional and lighter double-sider.

Wheels

Wheels take quite a pounding from the forces of acceleration, braking, the weight of the motorcycle, and irregular road surfaces and potholes. Wheels fall into two main categories—wire-spoked and cast.

A wire-spoked wheel (left) usually looks flimsy next to a cast sportbike item. The Oz item on this Aprilia (right) is the exception that proves the rule. Light weight with strength.

Wire-spoked wheels are less common these days but still find a place on some lightweight road bikes, customs, retros, and off-road machines. This last type of bike uses them because of their light weight and ability to take the punishment handed out by off-road riding, thanks in part to their inherent flexibility. BMW's GS series is one exception to the general road bike rule, although it must be said that the GS claims some off-road capability too. The BMW has spoked wheels cleverly laced to allow the use of tubeless tires—the spokes sit outboard of the tire bead. Moto Guzzi has adopted a similar system. Tubeless tires cannot be used on conventional spoked wheels because the air would leak out of the spoke holes.

Cast wheels

Cast wheels have become the norm for most bikes because they're light, strong, and easy to mass produce. It wouldn't take long for a modern high-powered superbike to break all the spokes in a wire wheel. In any case, modern radial tire designs are tubeless, so cast wheels are the obvious choice for most applications. Cast wheels are usually made from a one-piece casting incorporating hub, rim, and spokes, unlike the three separate elements of a wire-spoked wheel.

Like so many refinements on modern bikes, cast wheels came from the racing scene, where they were originally made from exotic alloys to cut down on weight. Another advantage was that the hubs could be made narrower than on spoked wheels, allowing more room for the fitment of disc brakes.

The cast wheels on mass-produced road-going machines are made of ordinary aluminum alloys, which are just as stiff but more robust and cheaper (if heavier) than magnesium. However, some top-end production sportbikes are now being graced with mag wheels and they are available as an aftermarket option.

The wheel deal

The most important thing for a wheel is that it's round. That's not being flippant. If a wheel runs out of true, perhaps because it's been damaged, handling can be upset, tires wear unevenly, and tubeless tires can deflate. Some runout is permissible, but if in doubt, have it checked out. Wire-spoked wheels can be trued up if the runout isn't too bad, and it is possible to have cast wheels repaired, provided the structural integrity of the wheel isn't compromised. But any chunks out of the rim, cracked cast spokes, or folds in the rim mean it must be replaced. Also, cast wheels can suffer fractures invisible to the naked eye in an impact, so if you have any doubts, have the wheels checked out by an engineering specialist.

It's important that you have the right tires on your wheels, that they are correctly aligned, and that the bearings are good. See the "Tires" and "Looking after your bike" sections for more information on these areas.

Lighten up

There's a big aftermarket wheel industry, ranging from builders of spoked wheels to companies making competition wheels out of exotic materials such as carbon fiber and magnesium and other light alloys. Apart from looking seriously trick, some of the latter can offer significant savings in unsprung weight. For a basic explanation of this, see the previous pages on swingarms. Another advantage is that light front wheels can help steering because there's less gyroscopic effect to overcome. To understand gyroscopic effect, next time you've got a wheel out of a bicycle, hold the axle and get a friend to spin it. Now move your hands up and down and side to side. You'll feel some strong forces at play. But as with most things in biking, there's a compromise. Heavier wheels help with straight-line stability, which is why Honda specifies a heavy tire for the Gold Wing.

Brakes

Unless you happen to be a drag racer, you'll appreciate the importance of decent brakes. Apart from a few lightweights, scooters, retros, and customs, it tends to be disc brakes all around these days—and even many of the bikes that feature drums on the back opt for discs up front.

Drum brakes

We'll keep it brief on the less common drum brakes. These work by forcing friction-material-lined shoes into contact with the steel- or iron-lined inside of the drum by way of a cable- or rod-operated cam or cams. Return springs pull the shoes clear of the drum when the brake levers are released.

They do their job adequately on low-powered, light bikes—provided the drum is true, the steel liner is not too worn, the shoes have got enough material on them, and the cable's in good shape.

Drum brakes are less efficient at dispersing heat than disc systems. Before the widespread use of disc setups, huge drums were used on race bikes and larger road bikes. Under hard use, these brakes would start to "fade" as the heat built up and braking efficiency was lost.

Drum brakes Simple in operation, but not up to the power, speed, and low maintenance requirements of most of today's bikes and riders.

WHEEL ROTATION

Pivot pin

Return spring

Trailing shoe

Brake drum

Wheel axle

Brake shoe

Backplate

Friction material

Cam

Brake lever

Brake off

WHEEL ROTATION

Friction lining forced against drum

Leading shoe

Brake on

Disc brakes

Disc brakes are far more efficient than drums. We have the aviation industry to thank for disc brakes, but it took a few decades for them to evolve into the hyper-powerful systems used on bikes today.

Pistons operated hydraulically in the calipers from the front, or rear master cylinders act on the steel backs of the friction pads, which squeeze the disc.

It's important that the calipers are designed to be rigid. If they were able to flex as the brakes were applied, their efficiency would diminish.

The most basic caliper has a single piston pushing one pad and slides to pull the other (fixed) pad against the disc. An opposed piston caliper has a pair or pairs of pistons pushing the pads. Multi-piston calipers are common on the front of bikes. Four piston (also more commonly known as four-pot) calipers are widely used. Kawasaki, for example, fits Tokico six-pots to some of its sportbikes. Certain aftermarket calipers have more still. But it's not just down to the number of pistons. Their area and their relationship (ratio) with the master cylinder at the lever is important too; likewise the area of the pads. The piston at the master cylinder has a small area, where the area of the piston(s) in the caliper is large. This gives rise to something called the "hydraulic multiplier effect," which means that relatively little force at the lever results in far greater forces at the caliper. Different-sized pistons are being used in certain individual calipers today to provide more progressive braking. When you stop applying the brakes, the disc "pushes" the pad away slightly and a rubber seal between the caliper and piston, shaped to twist a little as the piston moves out, pulls it back in again.

Multi-pot calipers allow longer, narrower pads to be used, meaning the area of the disc they operate on can be narrower and therefore lighter, reducing unsprung weight and gyroscopic forces (see "Swingarms" and "Wheels" for explanations of these).

Discs and pads

Discs are usually steel or iron. There's a limit to how narrow and thin they can be, because they have to be strong and there's a lot of heat to dissipate. On many modern designs, the disc can "float" slightly on its carrier to optimize pad contact and allow a little room for heat expansion, preventing warping.

Pad friction material is most commonly sintered metal these days because it works well in the wet—something early disc systems tended not to do. Different compounds are available for different applications. Hard brakers and trackday riders will have different requirements from touring riders, for example.

High-end race bikes feature carbon brakes (pads and discs), but the amount of heat that has to be in them to make them work means that they're no good for road bikes.

Likewise, full-on race compound pads might not work as well for standard brake setups on the road as they do on the track, although there are many aftermarket pads that offer performance superior to standard components for everyday use.

Other braking points

Some bikes feature linked braking systems, where application of either the front or rear brake will lead to complete or partial application of the other brake. This is not to every rider's tastes, many preferring individual control of the brakes, although the manufacturers do design these systems for balanced braking.

Other machines feature anti-lock braking systems, usually available as an optional extra, which allow riders to brake as hard as they like without skidding—in a straight line.

The efficiency of your disc brakes relies on correct maintenance of the brake system and periodic changes of the correct type of brake fluid. See your owner's manual or the "Looking after your bike" section of this book for more details.

Disc brakes Schematic of typical production system on left. Note small diameter yet high bulk of discs. PFM aftermarket system on right has skinny braking area of greater diameter, allowing light but long calipers making for high swept area yet low unsprung weight.

Chassis
accessories

There are aftermarket options for every chassis part we've discussed in this chapter, but there are other useful items you might want to consider too.

Grab rails Many bikes, especially sportbikes, are less than generous in passenger provision. There are aftermarket grab rails to give a passenger something to grab hold of if they don't want to get too intimate with the rider in the absence of standard-fit grab rails.

Huggers Most monoshock bikes have very little protection from road dirt and the elements for the rear shock and its linkages. A hugger mounted to the swingarm will reduce the amount of water and muck being thrown at the shock, swingarm, and back of the engine. Most replace the standard chainguard too. There's no problem of fit with better ones, but make sure cheaper items offer enough clearance for the tire and chain. An undertray for the rear seat unit makes that area easy to clean and keeps crud out.

Rearsets Hard road riders and trackday fanatics might find that standard footpegs don't offer enough ground clearance. Aftermarket rearsets mount the pegs and controls higher and farther back to help with this. Many have a huge range of adjustment for peg position to let riders set them for maximum comfort.

Frame Sliders *Motorcycle bodywork and cycle parts are expensive, so it's worth considering a set of sliders just in case the worst happens. Don't go for the cheap minimalist ones that will quickly disappear at the first hint of impact. Buy the type that bolt properly through frame and engine mount. This might mean some drilling of the fairing lowers, but it's worth it if they do their job and prevent your fairing and frame being ground off.*

Clip-ons *If you've gone for racy rearsets, you might find that the handlebars are now in the wrong place. Aftermarket clip-ons usually offer more adjustment than the standard bars fitted to your bike and there's often a weight benefit. Going the other way, riders who find the riding position of their bike too extreme might like to consider bar risers. Remember that cables and hoses might now be too long or too short. Check that everything can still operate freely.*

Screens *For bikes without screens, there are plenty of bolt-on options to offer a little weather protection. If you have a faired bike and find the standard screen inadequate, there are higher and double-bubble alternatives. But be aware that sometimes all these do is move the windblast to an equally uncomfortable part of your anatomy.*

Steering dampers *These hydraulic units are designed to prevent tank-slappers (where the bars wobble uncontrollably from side to side) and improve stability. Usually adjustable for damping, they connect between the frame and the forks. The chassis geometry of most modern bikes makes them sufficiently stable most of the time. But some bikes with more radical geometry for quick steering, particularly sportbikes, can suffer from shakes and wobbles when pushed hard. A decent damper reduces the problem. Some high-end sportbikes have them as standard, but there's a ready aftermarket supply for bikes that don't, or as improvements over the original equipment.*

Braided brake hoses *These are now fitted as standard on some bikes, but if not they make a huge difference in feel to disc brake setups, being less prone to expansion than conventional hoses. Stainless steel and Kevlar are popular materials for the braided outers of the hoses. The banjos that join the hose to the caliper are available in plated or stainless steel and alloy, but alloy should only be used on race bikes since road salt can cause dangerous corrosion.*

4

Looking after your motorcycle

Tools &
maintenance

Maintenance is vitally important. Just a few simple checks—even a quick glance before you ride—often makes the difference between catching a problem early, and expensive repairs later. It can even help to prevent an accident.

On any vehicle, things wear out, break, and come loose. After all, it's simply a collection of parts asked to do fairly extreme things. Just think about the forces acting on a bike and you can imagine how important it is to check that spindles are tight and there's oil in the engine. Of course, you're not going to prevent all failures with maintenance. The idea is simply to prevent the obvious ones so you can spend more time enjoying riding your bike and less time getting it fixed at the dealer.

A comprehensive list of daily and weekly checks

This is a reasonably comprehensive set of combination (open one end, ring the other) wrenches for bike work. Double up on the more popular sizes.

pressures, oil levels, and cable adjustments. You should know whether most of these things need adjusting as you ride.

Also, before you ride, just glance at the nuts and bolts you can see. Are any sticking out, indicating they're loose? It does happen, even on brand-new machines. If the engine takes longer and longer to start each time you ride, it's a sign that something is beginning to fail, even if it's just the battery. But catching it early means you won't be left stranded. So even with a little mechanical knowledge, you can save yourself money and have peace of mind that certain jobs have been done.

You'll find explanations and suggestions of what to check in the next few sections. By breaking the bike down into sections, looking after it seems less daunting. And as you become more familiar with working on bikes, you should be able to tackle more complicated jobs with ease. The first things you'll need are tools and it's worth making sure you have the right ones.

Tools are an essential part of looking after your bike. Good quality tools of the correct type will enable you to deal with jobs properly. You don't need tool chests and equipment reaching to the garage roof, but a few quality essentials will go a long way.

Wrenches

First and foremost are wrenches. A set ranging from 7 to 19mm is good enough to tackle the majority of the fasteners on most modern bikes, although you may want to get two 10, 12, and 13mm wrenches since they're popular sizes and sometimes it takes two to undo a component. Owners of some older British and American classics will need the appropriate imperial sizes for their machine. Buy combination wrenches—they have an open end and a ring end. There are numerous jaw and ring designs and the more expensive wrenches drive on the flats of the fasteners rather than the corners. But don't worry too much about this: quality and comfort are the priorities. Buy the best you can afford, and if you find over time that the most commonly used wrenches in the set are wearing badly, replace these with higher quality items. Garage sales are a great source of second-hand tools for people on a budget, and your money might be better spent there rather than on cheap and nasty new stuff. A couple of small adjustable wrenches are a worthy addition to your toolkit, but they're not as good as non-adjustable types because they are often more prone to slipping on fasteners, rounding them off.

This closed end drives on the flats of nut and bolt heads, reducing the risk of rounding off through better contact with the component.

This closed end offers more angles of attack, but drives on the corners, giving nuts and bolts a harder time.

Socket sets

A socket set is vital. As with wrenches, cheap stuff is a no-no, so the set you got free with ten bucks' worth of gas will not do the job. Quality is inferior and they're usually useless sizes anyway.

For bike work, 1/4, 3/8, and 1/2in are the most popular drive sizes, with sockets ranging from 6mm to 24mm in the best sets. Owners of old classics will again require imperial sets. Most sockets have a 12-point design, allowing the socket to fit in more positions and grip bolt heads and nuts snugly, avoiding rounding. However, a six-point design is better in some ways since it's more tolerant of fasteners that have already been slightly rounded. Once you've removed any such fasteners, it's a good idea to replace them with new ones—you might not be so lucky in removing them next time.

Allen, Torx, and spline bits are available to fit socket drives, as well as oil filter spinners. Torx and spline-headed bolts are also used occasionally, and you'll need the appropriate sockets.

Screwdrivers

It's worth buying good quality screwdrivers as the heads of screws are normally the first casualties of home servicing. Buy screwdrivers with good tips and comfortable handles. A selection of Phillips and flat-bladed screwdrivers is enough for most jobs. Be sure to use the screwdriver that has the best fit to the screw slots you're attacking. If you intend to strip engines, an impact screwdriver that can take sockets as well as screwdriver bits is handy.

Allen keys

Most modern bikes use Allen bolts to hold various things together, so a good set of keys is essential. Better than the classic key shape, consider getting a set of T-bars and some socket-Allen keys. You can use the socket keys to loosen tight bolts and the T-bars to remove them quickly. The most common sizes are 4–8mm, although try to go a little either side of this. Torx and spline keys will be required for some other fasteners.

Pliers

As well as a standard set of pliers, long-handled and needle-nosed pliers are extremely useful for working on bikes. They allow you to reach deep into the bike through limited gaps. A set of vice-grip pliers will also make life easier.

Torque wrenches

For reassembly, a torque wrench is essential to ensure fasteners are tightened to the correct figures as given in your workshop manual. This will avoid snapped fasteners, stripped threads, and distorted casings, or worse. There are two types: the beam type, which uses a pointer on a calibrated scale to show the applied torque; and the pre-set type, where the torque is set with an adjuster and the tool "gives" or clicks when the fastener is at the proper tightness. You'll need a torque wrench suited towards bike work (the majority of settings needed for bikes are lower than for cars). A tool with a range of 7–100Nm should suffice.

Tool care

Look after your tools and they'll give you years of service. A squirt of WD40 and a wipe with a rag after use is wise. Store them in a decent toolbox, kept in a dry place. If you try to apply some logic to which tool goes where in the box, you'll also save yourself hours of frustration hunting for the right tool.

Cleaning

Cleaning bikes is important. Apart from keeping your bike looking tidy and new for longer, which increases the amount of money you'll get when you resell it, this is a good way of spotting problems before they become too major.

A range of specialist bike-cleaning potions and implements. Beats a sponge and a bucket full of warm water and dishwashing liquid. Although that's better than nothing.

When race bikes are cleaned, the mechanics aren't just trying to keep the sponsors happy. As they clean the wheels, they'll be looking for cracks or dents. It's the same with the frame and other parts. Cleaning is the best way of spotting problems before they get serious.

The first thing to do is get rid of the thicker gunk, which, at the rear, normally comes in the form of old chain lube. Some paraffin or other degreaser on a rag will cut through this, and it must be rinsed away afterwards. Avoid using gas as a degreaser. Apart from being highly flammable, you don't want to get it on your skin. It can also attack some plastic and rubber parts on bikes. Applying degreaser by rag reduces the chances of it getting where it shouldn't, such as in the wheel bearings.

Fresh brake dust can normally be wiped off wheels easily. But old dust, and dust on the calipers, normally needs agitating, which is best done with a short-bristled paintbrush or old toothbrush. You can also get special brake dust removing sprays, which are pretty good. Some specialist wheel cleaning fluids are slightly corrosive. Make sure you don't spray or brush any on to unlaquered aluminum. Remember to clean dust from inside the caliper too, and use only brake cleaner or fresh brake fluid. Other solvents might attack the hydraulic seals.

The rest of the bike can be washed normally with water and detergent (dedicated products are better than dishwashing liquid) then polished. There's a bewildering array of specialized cleaning products on the market. But for general cleaning, you can do all these jobs with one product. Domestic general polishes like Simple Green are often ideal. They remove chain lube, dried-on flies, and brake dust and clean and polish at the same time—so you only have to do the job once. For dried-on flies and chain lube, spray it on liberally and leave for a minute or two. But try not to do it in conditions where the spray will dry. And remember to use a clean rag on your screen and paintwork. Whole screens have needed replacing because the rag used on them was the same one that cleaned a gritty area of bodywork.

If you're serious about cleaning, or your bike gets particularly filthy, you might want to invest in a power washer. But don't be too vigorous around wheel, head, swingarm, and shock bearings and linkages, since the grease can be forced out, which accelerates wear. The same goes for the chain, so be sure to lubricate it after jet washing.

With your bike cleaned, application of a good polish will bring out the shine, and silicon types claim to provide longer resistance to dirt buildup. Don't go too mad too often with paint-restoring polishes as these are usually mildly abrasive and you might wind up going through the paint. Use specialist polishes on bare aluminum and chrome, a favorite pastime of retro, cruiser, and classic enthusiasts.

Chain care

Chains do a lot of work in harsh conditions, so regular maintenance is essential. Ideally, chains should be inspected every 600 miles. Even a quick once-over and some lube is better than nothing and will increase chain life considerably. The three important chain care jobs are cleaning, adjustment, and lubrication.

It's important to keep chains clean because grit and other dirt sticks to the lube and acts as a grinding paste, speeding up the wear process. Clean the chain with something like paraffin to cut through built-up lube and then give it a good rinse. Don't leave the paraffin on the chain for ages, though.

Once clean, let the chain dry. If you spray on lube when it's still wet, you'll be trapping in moisture. It's important to know what type of chain you have fitted. Most bikes have O-ring chains, with rubber rings holding lubricant inside the rollers. These should be lubricated with O-ring chain lube. In this case, the lube will protect the outside of the chain and keep the O-rings supple and the grease inside the chain, rather than lubricating the pins.

No matter what type of chain, lube is best applied after a ride, when the chain is warm. This allows better penetration of the lube. When lubing chains, direct it so it hits in between the plates on both sides of the chain. Also, if you apply it to the lower run of the chain, centrifugal force will take care of lubing the outside. After a few minutes, wipe away any excess—it'll only fling off and make more mess elsewhere.

Automatic oilers are worth a mention because they save time and effort once fitted and extend chain life considerably. They also increase the time required between chain adjustments.

When adjusting chains, it's not only chain tension that's important. Wheel alignment is as crucial and should be checked carefully. Nearly all chain adjusters have some form of indicator, but if you have the time, it's worth double-checking wheel alignment using straight edges or a length of string because some adjusters can be out.

Checking chain tension and wear

To find out the correct tension and permissible chain stretch, check your manual.

With your bike upright (but not with someone sitting on it) and in neutral, push the bottom chain run down and measure the slack midway between the two sprockets. Rotate the rear wheel slightly and check again. Do this at several points along the chain because they wear unevenly, which leads to tight spots. Adjust for the correct tension at the tightest point on the chain.

If your chain is at, or close to, the end of its adjustment, it's worn out. This is best checked with the chain off the bike but can be done while it is still on. To do this, remove the chainguard and, with the chain taut, measure a number of links along the top run. Then see how the measurements compare to the spec in your manual. Rotate the rear wheel and

measure various sections of the chain in this way. Any kinking, frozen links, or missing O-rings mean that it's time for a new chain.

Check front and rear sprockets for signs of wear too. If either sprocket has teeth that appear bent or "hooked," do not be tempted to reverse the sprocket—this could lead to sudden failure because the teeth could break off. If either chain or sprockets are worn, replace as a set since one worn item will hasten the wear of the others.

Adjustment

Assuming that the chain and sprockets are still good, they can be adjusted. With the tightest point of the chain at the center of the bottom run and the bike supported upright (again without someone sitting on it, so either prop the bike securely or have someone hold it from the front), first loosen the axle bolt. Now loosen the locknuts for the sliding adjusters' screws and turn them equally until the chain is at the correct tension as specified in your manual. Check that the wheel alignment marks are in the same place on each side, and that everything is butting up as it should. If not, push the wheel forward or pull it back until they are. Check alignment marks and chain tension again. Once satisfied with everything, tighten the axle to the correct torque setting in your manual and tighten the locknuts. Make a final check of the chain tension before riding.

Things are slightly different on bikes with eccentric adjusters and single-sided swingarms, but correct chain tension is equally important. Refer to your manual for detailed advice on adjustment.

Remember that if a chain is too tight, it can cause havoc with gearboxes and bearings.

Direct chain lube so it gets between the plates on both sides of the chain. It's best to direct the spray at the lower run while the chain's warm, i.e., after a ride.

Look for the tightest point on the chain, then adjust as per the measurements in your manual. Some do it by feel. If in doubt use a ruler as shown here.

Brakes

The most important thing about any machine is its capacity to stop. That's why it's vital to keep brakes in good condition, so it stops when you ask it to. All bikes, no matter what their intended use, will use disc or drum brake systems or a combination of both.

Master cylinder reservoir
Check fluid level often, and if it decreases quickly check for leaks in the system. Murky fluid is contaminated and the system should be bled to replace it.

Brake hoses
Most bikes have lines with rubber-type outers that allow expansion over time leading to spongy brakes. Braided hoses are better.

Brake discs
Must be more than minimum thickness. They must also be unwarped or the brakes will shudder.

Calipers
Tend to attract road dirt impeding efficiency. Keep 'em clean with regular applications of brake cleaner. Check often for pad wear.

Inspection

The most important thing to check on disc or drum brake systems is the amount of friction material left on the pads or shoes (drum brakes have shoes, discs have pads). The material wears every time the brakes are applied and often wears faster than you might think.

You can check pads simply by looking through the caliper because many pads have wear indicators visible without the need to remove the calipers, but on multi-disc systems bear in mind that pads don't wear evenly. Check all the pads and never allow them to wear so far that the backing plate damages the discs. Drum brakes are harder to inspect and can sometimes require wheel removal, although most drums have wear indicators, which make life easier.

Replacing disc brake pads

Replacing brake pads means removing the calipers and pushing the pistons back with a piece of wood to accommodate the new pads. But before you do this, be sure to clean the pistons as best as you can. If you simply push them back, dirt and brake dust can be forced back into the caliper, which can stop the pistons withdrawing properly when you let go of the lever. A squirt of brake cleaner and a wipe is normally adequate.

But be aware that the fluid level can rise as the pistons go back and some may have to be siphoned off. Be careful not to get fluid on paintwork or plastics—it can attack them in seconds.

If necessary, add more brake fluid of the correct type as you pump the calipers up after refitting. Do not allow air to enter the system by letting the fluid level get too low, and make sure you have pumped the brake lever to put the pads back in contact with the disc before riding.

Other brake maintenance

Apart from the pads wearing, there is little else that requires attention. Hydraulic disc systems are self-adjusting, and the only thing to watch is the fluid level in the reservoir. The fluid should be renewed as per the service intervals suggested in your manual.

As the pads wear, more fluid will be taken into the system to take up the slack. If the level drops below the minimum, there is again a chance air will be drawn into the system, which reduces its effectiveness dramatically, making the controls feel spongy. Take a regular look at fluid level indicators on the master cylinders and never let the level drop below the minimum mark. If air does enter the system, the brakes will have to be bled properly.

As drum brake shoes wear, slack in the cables and brake rods will have to be taken up. Check the bike's manual for details of your system. Cables must be in good condition and must be kept correctly adjusted and lubricated.

Disc and drum surfaces need checking too. Discs should be inspected for cracks, as should drums. Discs and drums should also be measured for wear and distortion, and replaced if necessary. The minimum thicknesses are normally stamped on the parts, and can also be found in your manual.

On disc brake systems, the brake fluid, hydraulic seals, and hoses degrade over time and must be renewed in accordance with your bike's service schedule. Inspect hoses and unions regularly for signs of leaks and corrosion at the banjos. Brake fluid is hygroscopic and absorbs moisture from the atmosphere over time, impairing braking efficiency and giving a spongy feel at the lever or pedal. So don't neglect replacing it with the correct fluid at the specified intervals, and certainly no more than every couple of years, regardless of mileage. Always use new fluid from a sealed container.

Do not work on a bike's braking system unless you're confident you know what you're doing. Your Haynes manual shows you the correct procedures; for safety's sake follow them to the letter.

Basic disc caliper (left) and even more basic drum. Don't worry too much about what type of brakes your bike has, they're usually adequate. Pay more attention to maintenance.

Cables

Cables fulfill plenty of useful functions. Apart from where they've been superseded by hydraulic (disc brakes and some clutches) and electrical systems (some speedos, rev counters, chokes, and even throttles), cables operate a variety of components just as they have since the dawn of motorcycling.

Simple as cables are, they do require some care and attention for optimum performance. The most common killer is chaffing, where the cable flexes with the steering and wears through the outer casing. Once this happens, corrosion is likely to creep in.

Check for chaffing by inspecting the cables for flat spots. You should be able to see potential problems by turning the steering lock to lock and watching the cables. Cables sometimes fray and snap next to the nipple at the cable end. This is caused by the nipple not being able to rotate in the lever or throttle grip. Before replacing the cable, clean the hole in the lever/grip and smear the nipple with grease.

Routing

When routing cables, the straighter they are the better. Tight bends will make the cable harder to operate, increase the wear rate internally, and possibly cause the cable to stick. Bad routing can also cause a cable to operate when flexed. Before replacing a cable, make a note of how the original was routed. Inadvertent operation through bad routing is particularly a problem on the throttle and brakes. If you do fit new throttle cables, always move the bars from lock to lock with the engine running to make sure the throttle doesn't operate. We say throttle "cables" because almost all modern bikes have one cable to open the fuel supply (accelerator), complemented by one to close it (decelerator).

Cables should also be routed away from components that build up significant amounts of heat, such as exhaust pipes, or outers will melt and internal lubrication will be lost.

Free play on this R1's accelerator and decelerator cables is measured at the throttle itself. Too much or too little, and the cables will have to be adjusted.

Adjustments are made here by pulling the cable outer from the adjuster body. Adjuster and locknut can be seen clearly.

Here are the coarse adjusters at the carburetor end. When fitting cables it's best to take all the adjustment out of the fine adjusters and set the cables up using these coarse adjusters. Then as the cables stretch, the fine adjusters can be used to take up the slack.

Adjustment

Cables must be correctly adjusted for proper operation of controls. There must be adequate free play between the inner and outer so that controls aren't inadvertently operated when the bars are turned or the suspension extends and compresses. For correct cable adjustment, refer to your manual. Most are adjusted by simple barrel and locknut arrangements. In the case of cable clutches and front brakes, it is done by knurled wheel adjusters at the lever end for fine adjustment (as the cable stretches slightly in use), and other adjusters at the gearbox or brake end for coarser adjustment. Some throttle cables have fine adjusters near the twistgrip and coarser ones at the carb/throttle body end too.

Lubrication

As cables get older they get harder to use. This can be caused by fraying of the internal wire, or by dirt

buildup in the cable. If a cable is frayed, then it should be replaced immediately. If it is simply dirty, then lubricating the cable might displace some of the dirt and also make it easier to use.

It is possible to lubricate cables by creating a reservoir at one end and letting gravity draw lubricant through the cable. A quicker method is to use force. For less than $20, you can buy an adaptor that seals itself around one end of a cable. You then connect an aerosol lubricant (not chain lube) and squirt. The pressure expels dirt and ensures the cable is fully lubricated.

An alternative method is to use a pressure lubricator that is filled with light oil and operated by hand to force the oil through the cable. If an inner cable has a nylon liner, don't use oil to lubricate it. Oil can make the liner swell, and cause the cable to seize. Use a silicone spray instead.

Nipple

Oil

Plastic bag sealed around outer cable

Cable suspended vertically

Cable lubricated when oil drips from far end

Home-brewed cable lubricator (above). Pressure lubricator (far left) makes the job quick and easy, as does aerosol adaptor (left).

Without oil, engines will do considerable harm to themselves and won't run for long. Oil prevents damage by separating surfaces with a thin film, allowing parts to move past each other with minimal wear or friction.

Oil and filter change

Changing oil is easier on a warm engine because the oil is thinner. Remove the filler first to let the old lube flow more freely.

When removing the oil drain-plug, watch out for the initial gush of hot oil—and for other hot components, such as exhaust pipes. Make sure the drain tray you have under the sump is large enough to hold the used lube.

When fitting a filter, smear a small amount of clean oil evenly around the rubber seal and make sure no dirt has dropped on to the sealing face.

Fill the engine to the correct level with the bike upright—you'll get a false reading if the bike's on its side stand. It's important to use the right grade of engine oil, as specified by the manufacturer, so check your manual.

A large part of oil's role is a cleanup job in the motor. Over a period of time, an engine's oil will become contaminated with byproducts of the combustion process, including unburned fuel, moisture from condensation, and even coolant from the water jacket. All of this degrades its performance. These problems are on top of the degradation of the lubricant as it performs its basic job of cooling and lubing. Shearing forces break up the oil's molecular structure as it works hard to prevent the engine's key components from grinding themselves to bits, which is exactly what bits of metal flinging themselves at each other several thousands times a minute would inevitably do. Use the recommended oil for your bike as specified by the manufacturer. Your bike was designed to run with mineral, semi-synthetic, or fully synthetic oil. If you wish to upgrade, check with the bike's manufacturer or importer. Using the wrong oil can lead to clutch slip or worse. Don't be tempted to use cheap car oil of apparently the same specs. If you're unsure of what oil a second-hand bike's been filled with, drain and refill with semi-synthetic. You can go either way from there, depending on what's specified for the bike.

Making the change

Changing a bike's oil involves replacing the oil and filter. It's a good idea to replace them together, or at least fit a new filter every other oil change. Clogged filters can do as much damage as no oil, since they impede correct flow of lubricant, and fitting new filters without changing old oil won't improve the lube's performance.

Most bikes over 125cc have filters. Locations vary but are usually low down on the front or side of the engine for external filters, and underneath for internal ones. Nearly all external filters screw on. There are a number of strap and socket-drive tools available to remove them, and although it works,

stabbing them with a screwdriver is best avoided—as anyone who's had an eyeful of hot oil can testify. Replace filters with genuine bike manufacturer parts, or parts of the correct specification.

When disposing of used oil, it's your moral—and indeed legal—duty to dispose of it correctly. The drain in the street won't do. Transfer the contents of the oil drain pan into the container your new oil came in, and then take it to the recycling center, where they'll know what to do with it.

Most modern sump drain-plugs have a magnetic end to catch small pieces of metal generated by internal engine friction. These plugs should be wiped clean before refitting. It's also advisable to replace the sealing washer with a new one. These are often copper, or another soft metal such as aluminum, and sometimes they have a rubber insert. It's easy to be tempted to turn the washer upside down, assuming it will do the same job as a new one. But this ruse rarely works more than once, and what might start as a messy trickle can quickly turn into a messy and dangerous deluge if the drain plug decides to let go.

When first starting the bike after an oil refill, don't over rev it. It takes a while to fill the filter and build pressure in the system. Until then, you're relying on the oil film on components to keep the key parts safe, so give them an easy time. If the oil pressure warning light doesn't go out after a few seconds, stop the engine immediately. The problem might be down to a multitude of reasons after an engine rebuild. But after a refill, it's more likely to be because of adding too little oil or a major leak from filter or drain-plug—you did remember to install them, didn't you? We only ask because it's all too easy to forget—and then fail to notice the spreading puddle of fresh lube on the garage floor before realizing there is a problem. So never conduct maintenance in a rush. Let the bike idle for a few minutes before rechecking the oil level.

Oil drain cans/trays sold in car accessory shops are large enough to hold the contents of any bike sump.

Socket wrench driven tool for easy removal of external spin-on oil filters.

Cooling systems

Engines are not very efficient. Most of the energy released during combustion is transferred into heat and escapes into the engine or down the exhaust pipe. All the heat building up in the engine has to go somewhere, or the bike will overheat and the engine will be damaged. That's where cooling comes in.

Engines are either air-cooled or liquid-cooled. Liquid-cooling is the most popular choice these days, but is also more complicated. Air-cooled engines are very straightforward. The flow of air over the engine, as the bike moves along, takes the heat with it. Cylinders and heads have deep horizontal fins to help with heat dissipation. Problems only arise in very hot climates or if the machine is static or moving slowly for long periods. Some air-cooled bikes have oil-coolers, which look like radiators, to help the lubricant play a more efficient role in taking heat away from the engine. The old Suzuki GSX engines, as still used in the Bandit, are a good example of this. Suzuki describes them as air/oil-cooled.

In a liquid-cooled engine, coolant is pumped through a network of drillings in the motor's castings. Heat transfers to the coolant which then passes through a radiator where it is cooled. If for any reason the coolant doesn't flow, the engine will overheat.

The thermostat lets the engine get up to temperature before opening to allow the coolant to flow to the radiator.

Thermostats

A thermostat in the system gauges when the coolant is up to operating temperature and then allows it to flow to the radiator and the rest of the system. If it wasn't there, the bike would take a long time to warm up. If it fails to open, the engine will overheat. If you suspect the thermostat is faulty, it must be checked. If it is open at room temperature, then it has failed and must be replaced. To test that it opens, heat it in a pan of water and, using a thermometer, check the temperature at which it opens and compare the figure with the specs in your manual. Also check the amount it stays open after being heated at 194°F for a few minutes and, again, compare this figure with the specifications in your manual.

Temperature **sensors**

These are mounted in the engine block or cylinder head and are electrical devices whose resistance falls as coolant temperature rises. One brings the electric fan or fans behind the radiator into operation, while another is connected to the temperature gauge on your instrument cluster. On some models, one sensor combines these two operations.

If the fan stays on all the time, doesn't come on at all or cuts in at the wrong temperature, suspect the fan sensor (having first checked the fuse, if the fan doesn't operate at all). Likewise, if the temperature gauge doesn't work or gives clearly inappropriate readings, suspect the sensor.

Both of these sensors can be tested, but the procedure is more complex than for thermostats. See your manual.

Coolant

The most common problem with liquid-cooled engines is lack of coolant. Check the coolant is between the high and low levels on the expansion tank. Don't overfill the system because it has to vent as the liquid expands. Be sure to top off with the correct coolant for your bike.

Leaks reduce a system's effectiveness because coolant can escape and the system doesn't pressurize, reducing the coolant's boiling point. Check hoses and joints for leakage and inspect the radiator too. Sometimes leaks occur internally in the engine for various reasons and these are more serious. Coolant in the oil, which leads to a deposit that looks like mayonnaise, or oil in the coolant is a sign of this.

If the radiator fins have become clogged externally with road dirt or the odd unfortunate pigeon, air can't pass through it and the engine will run hot. Clean it using water from a hose in the opposite direction to which air flows, or, with care, a compressed air line.

Cooling systems are sometimes blocked by corrosion carried into the radiator. Although you can use water (distilled is far better than tap) in cooling systems, it's far better to use dedicated coolant or antifreeze of the correct type for your bike as both have corrosion inhibitors. Antifreeze also protects the system during cold weather. Plain water or coolant without antifreeze can turn into ice, which may lead to cracks in the system. When topping off a system filled with antifreeze, don't use just water on its own as this will dilute the antifreeze, lessening its efficiency. For maximum protection, coolant should be replaced every two years, although some systems are sealed for life.

Draining and refilling **the cooling system**

This is normally done in two stages and must always be done with the engine cold. Remove the pressure cap on the radiator to help the system drain. This must never be removed with the engine hot since scalding coolant and steam may escape and cause injury. When you're sure the engine is cool, remove the cap carefully and slowly with a rag over it. Remember that cooling systems are pressurized and there may still be enough pressure to spit coolant out at you.

Disconnect the hose from the neck of the radiator and use it to empty the expansion tank into a container sufficiently large to hold all the coolant in your bike's system. If any old coolant remains in the expansion tank, remove the tank and tip the fluid out. Next, loosen and remove the lowest coolant hose you can see on the engine. This should drain the radiator and engine. Often there are other drain plugs on the cylinder block and water pump cover. Remove these as well to allow any remaining coolant to escape.

Old coolant must be disposed of carefully, so check with the local authorities to find out the location of the nearest dump that can deal with it. Never leave it lying around. It's highly toxic so keep t away from children and animals. Wipe up any spills. Antifreeze is inflammable as well.

Refill the system, being careful to check for air by squeezing rubber hoses and possibly bleeding the pump if required. Check your manual for the complete procedure for your bike. Remember to fill the expansion tank to the correct level too.

The reservoir is usually mounted on the right-hand end of the radiator. Check that the coolant level is between the "FULL" and "LOW" level lines marked on the reservoir.

If the coolant level is low, remove any bodywork obstructing the filler cap. Remove the cap and top off the coolant with recommended coolant mixture. Fit the cap securely. Then re-install any bodywork.

Bearings

Compared to the engine, a bike's chassis is relatively free of bearings. But chassis bearings require more care than any in the engine, which have a ready supply of warm lubricant to look after them. There are four sets of chassis bearings to check—wheel, swingarm, rear suspension linkages and bushes, and headstock.

The wheel and headstock bearings are perhaps the most important. They're certainly the ones most capable of adversely affecting the handling characteristics. However, checking them is a fairly simple task, especially with a friend helping.

Wheel bearings

To check the front wheel bearings, you need to establish if there is any sideplay. The wheel should be free to spin forwards and backwards. To check bearings, set the steering in the straight-ahead position. If you don't have a front stand, ask a friend to lean the bike on its side stand until the front is off the ground. Things are even easier if your bike is equipped with a center stand—have your helper lean on the back of the bike.

Grab the wheel from one side and try pulling the top towards you while pushing the bottom end away. Any clicking or clunking is likely to be in the bearings, and the wheel should be removed to replace them. The procedure is the same for the rear wheel, and again it's easier if the wheel is off the ground by means of a rear stand, center stand (where fitted), or your ever-helpful friend pulling the bike over on its side stand.

Wheel bearings are usually the ball type, with one pressed into each side of the hub. Chain-drive bikes often have a third bearing in the cush/sprocket carrier assembly of the rear wheel. It's a similar deal with shaft-drive bikes, which often have an additional bearing or bearings in the bevel mechanism for the shaft drive. See your manual for bearing replacement procedure.Swingarm & rear suspension bearings

Swingarm bearings
As with most bearings, the swingarm's bearings or bushings are easiest checked with the help of a friend.

Wheel Bearings
Side-to-side wheel play or roughness when the wheel is rotated means the bearings are shot.

Swingarm & rear suspension bearings

On bikes with greasing points for these bearings, their life can be considerably lengthened by lubricating as per the maintenance schedule in your manual.

Checking the swingarm pivot bearings is a similar procedure to wheel bearings, but you won't be able to check them on a rear stand because you need to try to move the swingarm from side-to-side. Use your friend and the side stand trick. If the bearings feel suspect, you can carry out the same test with the suspension disconnected from the swingarm. To do this, though, the bike will have to be on a center stand, or stand under the engine or suspended from a beam in the workshop. It's much easier to feel swingarm pivot bearing play this way.

Swingarm bearings will either be bushings or needle, taper or ball roller type. Sometimes there's a combination of types. Refer to your manual for details on replacement.

The suspension linkage on monoshock bikes carries bushes or needle roller or ball bearings. To check for play in these, the rear wheel has to be off the floor with no weight on the swingarm. Grab the top of the rear wheel and pull it upwards. There should be no clunk or free play. Again, refer to your manual for details on replacement.

Steering bearings

Headstock, or steering, bearings need to be checked in two ways. With no weight on the front wheel (time to call on that friend again), move the bars left to right. On models fitted with a steering damper, make sure the damper is backed off to the position of least resistance. Steering action should be smooth and light. Any notchiness or tight spots are signs of bearing damage, and they should be replaced.

Because of the hammering these bearings get, they often work loose. Still with no weight on the front, get someone to push and pull quite hard on the bottom of the fork legs. While they do this, check for small movement by placing your fingers between the back of the top yoke and front of the tank. If you feel movement, the bearings are loose and need adjusting, the procedure for which will be in your manual.

Steering bearings benefit from regular regreasing and being correctly adjusted. The main types these days are taper roller and caged ball, although a few, mainly smaller, bikes still use uncaged balls. These are a laugh-a-minute to fit, since the grease you've used to hold them in the bottom race, while you get the bottom yoke back in, fails to do so, and the tiny balls drop on to the workshop floor.

Bearing markings reveal the bearing type. It can be cheaper to buy from a specialist bearing shop.

Rear suspension bearings and bushes These must be checked with the wheel off the ground and no weight on the swingarm.

Steering head bearings These need to be checked for side-to-side and front-to-back movement. Good handling relies on chassis bearings being in good condition and properly lubed and adjusted.

Electrical

Electrical systems are the most common cause of problems on bikes, so it pays to keep on top of them. Modern bike electrics are becoming increasingly complex but also increasingly strong, making the bikes we ride more reliable at the same time. Just a little bit of care will keep them that way.

Battery
Doesn't last forever, but keep topped-off, with de-ionized water, between the lines so the plates in each cell are covered in non-sealed types. Watch out for buildup of solids at the bottom of cells.

Battery

The obvious place to start is the battery. Unless you've got a modern sealed battery, you need to check it's filled to within the correct levels as indicated on the casing. If low, top it off with a little de-ionized water, but be careful not to get any acidic fluid from the battery on you or your clothes (or the bike). A battery that needs to be topped off too regularly indicates problems with the charging system. Refer to your manual for checks.

It is also well worth ensuring that the battery terminals are tight. These can work loose and cause problems that are hard to trace. A dab of petroleum jelly or battery grease prevents corrosion forming on the terminals and ensures a good connection.

Typically, a conventional lead acid battery will last for up to three years, provided it is properly maintained and kept charged up when the bike isn't in regular use.

Connectors

Satisfied that the battery is in good condition, it's worth checking the push-fit connectors that link the various electrical components. You'll find these all over most bikes, and if moisture gets in, it can cause failures. Split the connections and spray a little contact cleaner on the pins. Be careful not to spray bodywork or other plastic or painted components since they may be attacked by the contact cleaner.

Smearing a little bit of silicon grease or a squirt of WD40 on the connector body will make them easier to split next time.

Bulbs

Check that your lights work. That might sound simple but it's amazing how easy it is to forget this. It makes good sense before every ride to check headlight, taillights, and indicators and to apply both brakes to check that the brake light and its switches are working—and there are probably some meticulous souls that do. At the other end of the spectrum, there are riders who need to be told their rear light has failed and only notice headlight problems when they can't see in the dark. But it pays to be less slack than this because there is a major safety issue here.

Some bikes seem to get through rear bulbs at an alarming rate. This is often caused by vibration, so make sure the light unit is fitted correctly.

If you notice the direction indicator light on the dash flashing quicker than usual, it's normally a sign one or more of the indicator bulbs have failed.

When performing your routine checks of lights and indicators, give the horn a quick blast to make sure that's working too.

Fuses

The first thing to suspect when an electrical component stops working is its fuse. Bike fuse boxes are usually located in easily accessible places—under the seat, side panel, or inboard of the fairing.

There's usually a helpful key on a printed label in the lid of the fuse box to tell you which does what, and sometimes there's a couple of spares too. Some smaller machines just have a single fuse for all the systems, usually found near the battery.

A blown fuse often indicates a short circuit or a faulty electrical component, but sometimes they just blow for no reason, especially on bikes that vibrate a lot. If you replace a fuse and it blows again, the fault requires further investigation. Time to get the manual out. Some bikes use a resetable circuit breaker in place of the main fuse.

Switches

Handlebar switches are probably the most exposed electrical components—particularly on unfaired bikes. It is a good idea, once a year, to remove the switches, scrape away the corrosion, chase out the spiders, and apply a light smear of petroleum jelly to the switch components—metal and plastic.

A couple more tips

If you use a pressure washer to clean your bike, be careful not to blast electrical connectors or components. Although most systems are designed to be watertight, the force from a pressure washer may be too much.

Side stand kill-switches often get covered in chain lube from the front sprocket. Because they have the ability to kill the ignition system, keep them clean. Don't use solvent cleaners; simply wipe them with a rag and check that they operate freely and smoothly.

Connectors
A little bit of preventative maintenance will ensure they keep the electricity flowing to where it needs to go.

Bulbs do blow now and again, but usually through old age and sometimes vibration. If they persistently fail, there's a problem.

Fuses protect key components from electrical overload damage. Sometimes they just fail. Immediate failure on replacement shows there's a more serious fault.

Blown

Un-blown

Buying used

Street motorcycles fresh from the factory sold as new must meet state and federal requirements, but you also pay premium price. Buying used is a way to get the bike you want at a price you can better afford, but used bikes sold by private parties may not be legal—or roadworthy. To make sure you are getting your money's worth, you need to know what to look for. A filthy bike with cracked lenses and a dry chain has probably not had the best of maintenance. A newly waxed classic with fresh tires and an oil change might be a rare gem.

Brakes

- Raise each wheel off the ground, spin the wheel, operate then release the brakes, and check for binding of the wheel.
- Check brake discs for cracks and ensure they're securely mounted.
- Pad material should be checked visually on disc systems to ensure the pads aren't at their wear limit.
- Check drum brakes for correct operation of the lever and that the angle between operating cable or rod and the lever on the brake drum isn't too large with the brake applied.
- Brake hoses and their unions should be looked at for bulging in flexible pipes, and signs of corrosion and hydraulic fluid leakage elsewhere.
- Rear brake torque arms should be checked for security and that fasteners are held on by locknuts or cotter pins.
- ABS-equipped bikes have a self-check warning light in the instrument cluster, and you should check that this is working.
- It doesn't hurt to check braking efficiency, but it's nothing to worry about if you're satisfied your brakes are properly maintained.

Steering

- Raise the front wheel off the ground and turn the bars from lock to lock to check bars and switches don't scratch the tank or trap your thumbs. Busted lockstops and poorly fitted non-standard bars can cause problems here.
- At the same time, look for free steering movement without drag or notchiness caused by incorrectly routed cables or worn or badly adjusted head bearings.
- You should look for play in the head bearings by pulling on the bottom of the fork legs.
- Handlebars and controls must be securely mounted, as must the grips.

Wheels and tires

▶ Cast wheels must be free from cracks. Spoked wheels must have a full complement of spokes, free from corrosion, unbent and correctly tensioned.

▶ Rims must be unbent and true. Raise the wheels from the ground and spin to check for truth of tires and rims, and also to make sure they don't rub the mudguards, huggers, or suspension components.

▶ Wheel bearings should be checked for excessive wear. See the pages in the chapter on bearings for advice on how to check these.

▶ Check the tires for adequate tread and sidewall, and tread condition. See the section on tires for more information on this.

▶ Also check the tires to ensure they are the correct type and match each other front and rear. Tires must be suitable for road use. Anything marked otherwise may not be legal, so hand-cut slicks are out. Direction arrows on the tires should be checked too.

▶ Condition of wheel axles is another item on your agenda. The standard, self-locking or castellated nuts with split or R-clips should be tight and not rounded off.

▶ Consider checking wheel alignment. You can do this yourself by referring to this chapter's section on chains.

Final drive

▶ Chains and belts must be in good condition and at the correct tension. The rear wheel sprocket must be securely mounted on the hub. The overall condition of the sprocket should be checked too.

▶ On shafties, check the bevel unit for leaks that could lead to oil getting on to the rear tire.

General checks

▶ Remember, you're not trying to catch a crook. Just give the bike a careful inspection so you know what you are getting. So apart from the items detailed above, check that body panels, seat, mudguard, fairings, and major fasteners are secure.

▶ All footrests and controls must be securely mounted. Excessive corrosion on the frame or load-bearing components will result in a fall, so check these areas too.

▶ Finally, make sure the bike isn't damaged. In a crash, levers can get bent or broken, handlebars and signals can get bent, and bar ends, footpegs, cans, and mirrors can get scratched. Look for obvious crash damage, and some not so obvious. Check carefully to ensure the body panels all match.

Exhaust and Ride

▶ Exhaust must be securely mounted and not fouling the rear tire or rubbing on components.

▶ Start the bike and operate the throttle to ensure there are no holes or leaks in the entire system, including the collector box, where applicable.

▶ It's a good idea to spend a couple minutes listening to the bike run. Let it warm up. Make sure the throttle works properly, and snaps back when released. Listen for engine noises you wouldn't normally

associate with a properly-maintained motorcycle. Ask the owner to give you a ride, or take it out yourself.

▶ When riding, pay attention to the stability of the motorcycle. Investigate any strange sensations like wobbling, weaving, or vibrating. Run the motor through the rpm range and all the gears to make sure that response is smooth and predictable. Test the brakes a few times to make sure they're not spongy or warped. If you're not sure how that particular bike should "feel," bring along a friend, or better yet, an experienced mechanic who knows what to look for.

Rear suspension

▶ Have an assistant hold the front of the bike while you bounce the rear with the bike off its stand. You are looking for adequate damping in the rear shock(s) while checking that nothing is rubbing.

▶ Take a close look at the shock(s) to check the damper rod(s) aren't corroding and the damping oil isn't leaking.

▶ The swingarm's pivot bearings should be checked, with the rear wheel raised off the ground, by pulling it from side-to-side. At the same time, the rear wheel should be pulled up by its highest point to check for wear in the suspension linkages.

Lights, indicators, horn, and reflectors

▸ Headlight and taillight must both operate with the switch in high and low beam positions.
▸ With the switch in the parking light position, the signals and taillights should light up.
▸ Indicators should flash at the proper speed and the indicator lights and switch must work properly. If your bike has a hazard warning system, all four indicators should must when it's operated.
▸ The brake light must come on when each brake is operated. Check that the stop lamp works properly for both front and rear brakes.
▸ The horn should have a continuous tone and sufficient volume.
▸ The headlight beam must be at the right height, but it's adjustable and easily fixed. If you think yours is out, check it as per the diagram on this page. Draw a horizontal line on the garage wall at the same height as the center of your headlight and position the bike as per the distance and angle shown in the diagram. Draw a vertical mark in line with the centerline of the bike. Now take the bike off its stand and sit on it. When the headlight is dipped, the beam on the wall should fall below the horizontal and to the right of the vertical lines.

Front suspension

▸ With the bike off the stand, it's time to sit on it, squeeze the front brake, and pump the forks up and down to check they don't bind and there's adequate damping.
▸ Fork seals and the stanchion area next to them should be checked, the former for leaks and the latter for pitting or corrosion.

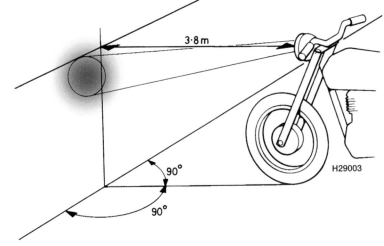

3·8 m

90°

90°

H29003

Storage

Unless you're commuting to and from work on your bike, it will probably spend a few months of the year in storage. But storing a bike isn't just a case of putting it in the shed and forgetting about it—not if you want it to be in a decent state when summer returns.

Motorcycles are highly susceptible to corrosion caused by road salt, because their parts are so exposed. Corrosion can start in a matter of days, and is hard to halt. So give the bike a good wash before you put it away, and make sure it's completely dry before it's consigned to the garage.

If the bike is faired, remove the fairing to reach the awkward places underneath. A firm-bristled bottlebrush makes life easier and saves your knuckles, although using a pressure washer is perhaps the most convenient and effective method. Just remember not to be too vigorous around steering, suspension and wheel bearings, and electrical components. Lube the chain afterwards too.

Coat the piston bores and rings with oil by removing the spark plugs and squirting about a teaspoon of oil down each spark plug hole. Put the plugs back in and crank the engine over with the kick start (where fitted), or on the electric start with the kill-switch off. Some bikes only allow the engine to turn with the kill-switch on so the plugs will have to be grounded against the cylinder head—far enough away from the spark plug holes to avoid igniting any fuel vapor in the bores.

Consider draining the gas or, at the very least, turn the fuel tap off and run the bike until it stops. This prevents gas residue building up in the carbs and blocking small orifices. Otherwise, turn off the fuel tap and drain the carbs by way of the drain screws at the bottom of the float-bowls. If your bike is going to be off the road for a long time, you might want to add fuel stabilizer to the gas. Otherwise, gas can go bad in storage and you'll need to replace it come springtime. Remember to dispose of old fuel properly.

Completely drained tanks can corrode internally if left for a long time. Remove the tank, pour half a quart of engine oil into it and agitate the tank to coat the inside with oil. Remember to clean the oil out before refilling the tank with petrol. Alternatively, spray the inside of the tank with WD40 or similar.

Air intakes and exhaust orifices can be plugged or covered in plastic to prevent buildup of condensation. Run the bike until it's hot, allow to cool, then cover.

Most batteries, even new ones, will discharge if the bike is unused over the winter. The problem is worse if the bike is alarmed, no matter how small the drain. A trickle charger helps keep batteries topped off, without damaging them. It's best to remove the battery from the bike and keep it in a place where there's no danger of it freezing.

If it's an unsealed type, ensure there's enough electrolyte in it.

If the bike is liquid-cooled, check it has antifreeze in. It takes only one freezing night to do expensive damage. Corrosion inhibitors in the antifreeze will help prevent internal damage to the cooling system. And if the bike is chain driven, make sure it's lubed—a rusty chain wears faster. While lubing, you might consider a light coat of WD40 or similar on

the wheel rims if they're chrome, and on fork sliders and other exposed metal parts. Remember not to spray the brake discs, however.

Finally, check tire pressures. A bike standing for several months on flat tires is likely to deform them so badly that they lose their shape, or even worse, develop splits. Deflate by no more than 5–10psi. If your bike has a center stand, put it on that with blocks of wood under each wheel to save them from damp. If possible, store the bike on paddock stands so that the wheels are off the ground. If you haven't got any such stands, rotate the wheels periodically so they're not standing on the same section of tire.

Tempting as it is to start the engine every so often, try not to unless you intend to let it get up to operating temperature. If the engine isn't thoroughly warm, condensation is likely to form in the engine and contaminate the oil, possibly causing internal corrosion.

Trickle chargers keep batteries in optimum condition.

Disconnect the battery while your bike's in storage.

If a cable-operated clutch sticks in storage, tie the lever back to see if it frees.

Is your bike **legal?**

License plate

Having a license plate usually means your bike is street legal. This means you've got a headlight with high and low beam, a red tail light with a stop lamp, brakes, exhaust, and a rearview mirror. Some states also require a horn, turn signals, speedometer/odometer, a periodic inspection, daytime headlight use, and handlebar height restrictions.

Exhaust pipe

Aftermarket exhaust cans are the most popular thing people fit, either because they want the extra noise and performance, or simply because after a crash it's a cheaper alternative to buying a replacement stock silencer. However, unless the exhaust meets government noise requirements and is marked to say so, it is illegal for road use. Most race cans have a "not for road use" marking and removing this doesn't make it legal.

Headlight cover

The law says forward-facing lights should be white and rear-facing lights should be red. Any departure from this is illegal. Headlight covers are often fitted to color match with the bodywork. These are illegal. Clear covers are useful because they prevent costly stone damage to the headlight.

Bigger tires

Although not illegal, fitting larger or smaller tires than those recommended by the manufacturer is inadvisable. More than anything, it will affect the bike's handling, and there's a chance your insurance company could use it as an excuse not to pay out in an accident.

Bodywork

There is no law against what color your bike can be, although you couldn't get away with having it painted like a police bike. It's generally frowned upon to have race-like numbers on it.

Passengers

So long as the bike was designed to take passengers, and so long as the passenger can sit with his or her feet on the footrests, it's okay for that person to ride along. The only real legal requirements are that they are large enough and that you're licensed to carry them. Some insurance policies exclude cover for passengers, so it's worth checking your own policy.

Trouble shooting

When things go wrong, as they sometimes do, don't panic. A motorcycle is a mechanical entity and as such is governed by rules of basic engineering and mechanics. By applying a little logic, it's reasonably easy to drill down to the root of a problem, and even if your own mechanical skills or workshop resources don't stretch to it, you'll be able to point the guys in the shop in the right direction.

To help you see the trees from the forest, here is some basic fault-finding material that will at least guide you in the right direction. Two-stroke riders can ignore any references to valves and camshafts, of course, but the rest of the material pretty much applies regardless of engine type. Remember this is a general guide, so for specific treatment of problems refer to the owner's manual for your bike.

Engine doesn't start or is difficult to start

Starter motor doesn't rotate

Engine kill switch OFF.
Fuse blown. Check main fuse and starter circuit fuse. See your Haynes manual.

Battery voltage low.
Check and recharge battery.

Starter motor defective.
Make sure the wiring to the starter is secure. Make sure the starter relay clicks when the start button is pushed. If the relay clicks, then the fault is in the wiring or motor.

Starter relay faulty.
See your Haynes manual.

Starter switch not contacting.
The contacts could be wet, corroded, or dirty. Disassemble and clean the switch. See your Haynes manual.

Wiring open or shorted.
Check all wiring connections and harnesses to make sure that they are dry, tight, and not corroded. Also check for broken or frayed wires that can cause a short to ground (earth). Refer to the wiring diagram in your Haynes manual.

Ignition (main) switch defective.
Check the switch according to the procedure in your Haynes manual. Replace the switch with a new one if it is defective.

Engine kill switch defective.
Check for wet, dirty, or corroded contacts. Clean or replace the switch as necessary.

Faulty neutral, side stand, or clutch switch.
Check the wiring to each switch and the switch itself according to the procedures in your Haynes manual.

Starter motor rotates but engine does not turn over

Starter clutch defective.
Inspect and repair or replace. See your Haynes manual.

Damaged idle/reduction or starter gears.
Inspect and replace the damaged parts. See your Haynes manual.

Starter works but engine won't turn over (seized).
Seized engine caused by one or more internally damaged components. Failure due to wear, abuse, or lack of lubrication. Damage can include seized valves, followers, camshafts, pistons, crankshaft, connecting rod bearings, or transmission gears or bearings. See your Haynes manual for engine disassembly.

No fuel flow

No fuel flow

No fuel in tank.

Fuel tank breather hose obstructed.

Fuel tap filter or in-line filter (carburetor models) or fuel pump assembly filter (fuel injection models) clogged.
Remove the tap or pump and clean or renew the filter. See your Haynes manual.

Fuel line clogged.
Pull the fuel line loose and carefully blow it through.

Float needle valve clogged (carburetor models).
For all of the valves to be clogged, either a very bad batch of fuel with an unusual additive has been used, or some other foreign material has entered the tank. Many times after a machine has been stored for many months without running, the fuel turns to a varnish-like liquid and forms deposits on the inlet needle valves and jets. The carburetors should be removed and overhauled if draining the float chambers doesn't solve the problem.

Fuel pump or relay (fuel injection models) faulty.
Check the fuel pump and relay. See your Haynes manual.

Engine flooded (carburetor models).
Float height too high. Check as described in your Haynes manual.

Float needle valve worn or stuck open.
Dirt, rust, or other debris can cause the valve to seat improperly, causing excess fuel to be admitted to the float chamber. In this case, the float chamber should be cleaned and the needle valve and seat inspected. If the needle and seat are worn, then the leaking will persist and the parts should be replaced.

Starting technique incorrect.
Under normal circumstances (i.e., if all the carburetor functions are sound) the machine should start with little or no throttle. When the engine is cold, the choke should be operated and the engine started without opening the throttle. When the engine is at operating temperature, only a very slight amount of throttle should be necessary. If the engine is flooded, turn the fuel tap OFF (where fitted) and hold the throttle open while cranking the engine. This will allow additional air to reach the cylinders. Remember to turn the fuel tap back ON after the engine starts.

Engine flooded (fuel injection models).
Faulty pressure regulator—if it is stuck closed there could be excessive pressure in the fuel rail. Check as described in your Haynes manual.

Injector(s) stuck open, allowing a constant flow of fuel into the engine.
Check as described in your Haynes manual.

Starting technique incorrect.
See advice as for carbureted bikes. But remember some fuel injected bikes have no choke lever and most have no manually operated fuel tap.

No spark or weak spark

Ignition switch OFF.

Engine kill switch turned to the OFF position.

Battery voltage low.
Check and recharge the battery as necessary. See your Haynes manual.

Spark plugs dirty, defective, or worn out.
Locate reason for fouled plugs using spark plug condition chart and follow the plug maintenance procedures. See your Haynes manual.

Spark plug caps faulty.
Check condition. Replace if cracks or deterioration are evident. See your Haynes manual.

Spark plug caps not making good contact.
Make sure that the plug caps fit snugly over the plug ends.

Ignition control unit (carburetor models) or ECM (fuel injection models) defective.
Check the unit, referring to your Haynes manual for details.

Pulse generator defective.
Check the unit, referring to your Haynes manual for details.

Ignition coils defective.
Check the coils, referring to your Haynes manual.

Ignition or kill switch shorted.
Usually caused by water, corrosion, damage, or excessive wear. The switches can be disassembled and cleaned with electrical contact cleaner. If cleaning does not help, replace the switches referring to your Haynes manual.

Wiring shorted or broken between:
a) Ignition (main) switch and engine kill switch (or blown fuse)
b) Ignition control unit or ECM and engine kill switch
c) Ignition control unit or ECM and ignition coils
d) Ignition coils and spark plugs
e) Ignition control unit or ECM and pulse generator.

Make sure that all wiring connections are clean, dry, and tight.
Look for chafed and broken wires.

Compression low

Spark plugs loose.
Remove the plugs and inspect their threads. Reinstall and tighten to the specified torque. See your Haynes manual.

Cylinder heads not sufficiently tightened down.
See your Haynes manual. If a cylinder head is suspected of being loose, then there's a chance that the gasket or head is damaged if the problem has persisted for any length of time.

Incorrect valve clearance.
Check and adjust the valve clearances as per your manual.

Cylinder and/or piston worn.
Excessive wear will cause compression pressure to leak past the rings. This is usually accompanied by worn rings as well. A top-end overhaul will be required.

Piston rings worn, weak, broken, or sticking.
Broken or sticking piston rings usually indicate a lubrication or carburetion problem that causes excess carbon deposits or seizures to form on the pistons and rings. Top-end overhaul will again be necessary.

Piston ring-to-groove clearance excessive.
This is caused by excessive wear of the piston ring lands. Piston and ring replacement will be called for.

Cylinder head gasket damaged.
If a head is allowed to become loose, or if excessive carbon buildup on the piston crown and combustion chamber causes extremely high compression, the head gasket may leak. Retorquing the head is not always sufficient to restore the seal, so gasket replacement is needed too.

Cylinder head warped.
This is caused by overheating or improperly tightened head bolts. Machine shop resurfacing or head replacement and a new gasket will be needed.

Valve spring broken or weak.
Caused by component failure or wear; the springs must be replaced.

Valve not seating properly.
This is caused by a bent valve (from over-revving or improper valve adjustment), burned valve or seat (improper carburetion), or an accumulation of carbon deposits on the seat (from carburetion or lubrication problems). The valves must be cleaned and/or replaced and the seats serviced if possible or replaced by an engineering shop.

Stalls after starting

Improper choke action (carburetor models).
See your Haynes manual.

Ignition malfunction.
See your Haynes manual.

Carburetor or fuel injection system malfunction.
See your Haynes manual.

Fuel contaminated.
The fuel can be contaminated with either dirt or water, or can change chemically if the machine is allowed to sit for several months or more. Drain the tank and float chambers. Also check that fuel can flow freely.

Intake air leak.
Check for loose carburetor or throttle body-to-intake manifold connections, loose or missing vacuum gauge adapter screws or hoses, or loose carburetor tops.

Engine idle speed incorrect.
Turn idle adjusting screw until the engine idles at the specified rpm in your manual. On fuel injection models, check other components as specified in your Haynes manual.

Rough idle

Ignition malfunction.
See your Haynes manual.

Idle speed incorrect.
See your Haynes manual.

Carburetors or throttle bodies not synchronized.
Adjust with vacuum gauge or manometer set as described in your Haynes manual.

Carburetor or throttle body or fuel injection system malfunction.
See your Haynes manual.

Fuel contaminated.
The fuel can be contaminated with either dirt or water, or can change chemically if the machine is allowed to sit for several months or more. Drain the tank and float chambers as per your manual.

Intake air leak.
Check for loose carburetor or throttle body-to-intake manifold connections, loose or missing vacuum gauge adaptor screws or hoses, or loose carburetor tops.

Air filter clogged.
Clean or replace the air filter element.

Poor running at low low speeds

Spark weak

Battery voltage low.
Check and recharge battery.

Spark plugs fouled, defective or worn out.

Spark plug cap defective.
See your Haynes manual.

Spark plug caps not making contact.

Incorrect spark plugs.
Wrong type, heat range, or cap configuration. Check and install correct plugs.

Ignition control unit (carburetor models) or ECM (fuel injection models) defective.
Check as per instructions in your manual.

Pulse generator defective.

Ignition coils defective.

Fuel/air mixture incorrect Carburettor mods

Pilot screws out of adjustment.
See your Haynes manual.

Pilot jet or air passage clogged.
Remove and overhaul the carburetors. See your Haynes manual.

Air bleed holes clogged.
Remove carburetor and blow out all passages. See your Haynes manual.

Fuel level too high or too low.
Check the float height as detailed in your manual.

Carburetor intake manifolds loose.
Check for cracks, breaks, tears or loose clamps. Replace rubber intake manifold joints if split or cracked.

Fuel/air mixture incorrect Fuel injection models

Fuel injection system malfunction.
See your Haynes manual.

Fuel injector clogged.
See your Haynes manual.

Fuel pump or pressure regulator faulty.

Throttle body intake manifolds loose.
Check for cracks, breaks, tears, or loose clamps. Replace rubber intake manifold joints if split or cracked.

Fuel/air mixture incorrect All models

Air filter clogged, poorly sealed, or missing.

Air filter housing poorly sealed.
Look for cracks, holes, or loose clamps and replace or repair defective parts.

Fuel tank breather hose obstructed.

Compression low

Spark plugs loose.
Remove the plugs and inspect their threads. Reinstall and tighten to the specified torque in your manual.

Cylinder heads not sufficiently tightened down.
If a cylinder head is suspected of being loose, then there's a chance that the gasket and head are damaged if the problem has persisted for any length of time. The head bolts should be tightened to the proper torque in the correct sequence described in your manual.

Incorrect valve clearance.
This means that the valve is not closing completely and compression pressure is leaking past the valve. Check and adjust the valve clearances.

Cylinder and/or piston worn.
Excessive wear will cause compression pressure to leak past the rings. This is usually accompanied by worn rings as well. A top end overhaul is necessary.

Piston rings worn, weak, broken, or sticking.
Broken or sticking piston rings usually indicate a lubrication or carburetion problem that causes excess carbon deposits or seizures to form on the pistons and rings. Top-end overhaul is necessary.

Piston ring-to-groove clearance excessive.
This is caused by excessive wear of the piston ring lands. Piston and probably ring replacement is necessary.

Cylinder head gasket damaged.
If a head is allowed to become loose, or if excessive carbon buildup on the piston crown and combustion chamber causes extremely high compression, the head gasket may leak. Retorquing the head is not always sufficient to restore the seal, so gasket replacement is necessary.

Cylinder head warped.
This is caused by overheating or improperly tightened head bolts. Machine shop resurfacing or head replacement is necessary.

Valve spring broken or weak.
Caused by component failure or wear; the springs must be replaced.

Valve not seating properly.
This is caused by a bent valve (from over-revving or improper valve adjustment), burned valve or seat (improper carburetion) or an accumulation of carbon deposits on the seat (from carburetion, lubrication problems). The valves must be cleaned and/or replaced and the seats recut or replaced if possible.

Poor acceleration

Carburetors or throttle bodies leaking or dirty.
Overhaul them.

Fuel injection system malfunction.
Faulty fuel pump, or pressure regulator (fuel injection models).

Timing not advancing.
The pulse generator or the ignition control unit or ECM may be defective. If so, they must be replaced with new ones, as they can't be repaired.

Carburetors or throttle bodies not synchronized.
Adjust them with a vacuum gauge set or manometer.

Engine oil viscosity too high.
Using a heavier oil than that recommended can damage the oil pump or lubrication system and cause drag on the engine.

Brakes dragging.
Usually caused by debris that has entered the brake piston seals, or from a warped disc or bent wheel spindle. Repair and replace as necessary.

Poor running or no power at high speed

Firing incorrect

Air filter restricted.
Clean or replace filter.

Spark plugs fouled, defective, or worn out.

Spark plug caps defective.

Spark plug caps not in good contact.

Incorrect spark plugs.
Wrong type, heat range, or cap configuration. Check and install correct plugs listed in your manual.

Ignition control unit or ECM defective.

Ignition coils defective.

Fuel/air mixture incorrect
Carburettor models

Main jet clogged.
Dirt, water, or other contaminants can clog the main jets. Clean the fuel tap filter, the in-line filter, the float chamber area, and the jets and carburetor orifices.

Main jet wrong size.
The standard jetting is for sea level atmospheric pressure and oxygen content.

Throttle shaft to carb body clearance excessive.
Check manual for inspection and renewal.

Air bleed holes clogged.
Remove carburetor and blow out all passages.

Fuel level too high or too low.
Check the float height.

Carburetor intake manifolds loose.
Check for cracks, breaks, tears or loose clamps. Replace rubber intake manifold joints if split or cracked.

Fuel pump, where fitted, faulty.

Fuel/air mixture incorrect
Fuel injection models

Fuel injection system malfunction.

Fuel injector clogged.

Fuel pump or pressure regulator faulty.

Throttle body intake manifolds loose.
Check for cracks, breaks, tears or loose clamps. Replace rubber intake manifold joints if split or cracked.

Fuel/air mixture incorrect
All models

Air filter clogged, poorly sealed or missing.

Air filter housing poorly sealed.
Look for cracks, holes, or loose clamps and replace or repair defective parts.

Fuel tank breather hose obstructed.

Compression low

Spark plugs loose.
Remove the plugs and inspect their threads. Reinstall and tighten to the specified torque.

Cylinder heads not sufficiently tightened down.
If a cylinder head is suspected of being loose, then there's a chance that the gasket and head are damaged if the problem has persisted for any length of time. The head bolts should be tightened to the proper torque in the correct sequence.

Incorrect valve clearance.
This means that the valve is not closing completely and compression pressure is leaking past the valve. Check and adjust the valve clearances.

Cylinder and/or piston worn.
Excessive wear will cause compression pressure to leak past the rings. This is usually accompanied by worn rings. A top-end overhaul is necessary.

Piston rings worn, weak, broken, or sticking.
Broken or sticking piston rings usually indicate a lubrication or carburetion problem that causes excess carbon deposits or seizures to form on the pistons and rings. Top-end overhaul is necessary.

Piston ring-to-groove clearance excessive.
This is caused by excessive wear of the piston ring lands. Piston and probably ring replacement is necessary.

Cylinder head gasket damaged.
If a head is allowed to become loose, or if excessive carbon buildup on the piston crown and combustion chamber causes extremely high compression, the head gasket may leak. Retorquing the head is not always sufficient to restore the seal, so gasket replacement is necessary.

Cylinder head warped.
This is caused by overheating or improperly tightened head bolts. Machine shop resurfacing or head replacement is necessary.

Valve spring broken or weak.
Caused by component failure or wear; the springs must be replaced.

Valve not seating properly.
This is caused by a bent valve (from over-revving or improper valve adjustment), burned valve or seat (improper carburetion) or an accumulation of carbon deposits on the seat (from carburetion or lubrication problems). The valves must be cleaned and/or replaced and the seats serviced or replaced if possible.

Knocking or pinking

Carbon buildup in combustion chamber.
Use of a fuel additive that will dissolve the adhesive bonding the carbon particles to the crown and chamber is the easiest way to remove the buildup. Otherwise, the cylinder heads will have to be removed and decarbonized. Rare with modern fuels.

Incorrect or poor quality fuel.
Old or improper grades of fuel can cause detonation. This causes the piston to rattle, thus the knocking or pinging sound. Drain old fuel and always use the recommended fuel grade.

Spark plug heat range incorrect.
Uncontrolled detonation indicates the plug heat range is too hot. The plug in effect becomes a glow plug, raising cylinder temperatures. Install the proper heat range plug.

Improper air/fuel mixture.
This will cause the cylinders to run hot, which leads to detonation. Clogged jets or an air leak can cause this imbalance.

Miscellaneous causes

Throttle valve doesn't open fully.
Adjust the throttle grip free play.

Clutch slipping.
May be caused by loose or worn clutch components. Refer to your manual for clutch overhaul procedures.

Timing not advancing
Faulty ignition control unit or ECM.

Engine oil viscosity too high.
Using a heavier oil than recommended can damage the oil pump or lubrication system and cause drag on the engine.

Brakes dragging.
Usually caused by debris that has entered the brake piston seals, or from a warped disc or bent axle. Repair and replace as necessary.

Overheating

Engine overheats

Coolant level low.
Check and add coolant.

Leak in cooling system.
Check cooling system hoses and radiator for leaks and other damage. Repair or replace parts as necessary.

Thermostat sticking open or closed.
Check and replace.

Faulty radiator cap.
Remove the cap and have it pressure tested.

Coolant passages clogged.
Have the entire system drained and flushed, then refill with fresh coolant.

Water pump defective.
Remove the pump and check the components.

Clogged radiator fins.
Clean them by blowing compressed air through the fins in the reverse direction of airflow.

Cooling fan or fan switch fault.

Firing incorrect

Spark plugs fouled, defective or worn out.

Incorrect spark plugs.

Ignition control unit or ECM defective.

Pulse generator faulty.

Faulty ignition coils.

Fuel/air mixture incorrect
Carburettor models

Main jet clogged.
Dirt, water, or other contaminants can clog the main jets. Clean the fuel tap filter, the in-line filter, the float chamber area, and the jets and carburetor orifices.

Main jet wrong size.
The standard jetting is for sea level atmospheric pressure and oxygen content.

Throttle shaft-to-carburetor body clearance excessive.

Air bleed holes clogged.
Remove carburetor and blow out all passages.

Fuel level too high or too low.
Check the float height.

Carburetor intake manifolds loose.
Check for cracks, breaks, tears or loose clamps. Replace rubber intake manifold joints if split or cracked.

Fuel pump faulty.

Fuel/air mixture incorrect
Fuel injection models

Fuel injection system malfunction.

Fuel injector clogged.

Fuel pump or pressure regulator faulty.

Throttle body intake manifolds loose.
Check for cracks, breaks, tears, or loose clamps. Replace rubber intake manifold joints if split or cracked.

Fuel/air mixture incorrect
All models

Air filter clogged, poorly sealed, or missing.

Air filter housing poorly sealed.
Look for cracks, holes, or loose clamps and replace or repair defective parts.

Fuel tank breather hose obstructed.

Compression too high

Carbon buildup in combustion chamber.
Use of a fuel additive that will dissolve the adhesive bonding the carbon particles to the piston crown and chamber is the easiest way to remove the buildup. Otherwise, the cylinder heads will have to be removed and decarbonized.

Improperly machined head surface or installation of incorrect gasket during engine assembly.

Engine load excessive

Clutch slipping.
Can be caused by damaged, loose, or worn clutch components. Refer to your manual for overhaul procedures.

Engine oil level too high.
The addition of too much oil will cause pressurization of the crankcase and inefficient engine operation. Check specifications and drain to proper level.

Engine oil viscosity too high.
Using a heavier oil than recommended can damage the oil pump or lubrication system as well as cause drag on the engine.

Brakes dragging.
Usually caused by debris that has entered the brake piston seals, or from a warped disc or bent axle. Repair and replace as necessary.

Lubrication inadequate

Engine oil level too low.
Friction caused by intermittent lack of lubrication or from oil that is overworked can cause overheating. The oil provides a definite cooling function in the engine. Check the oil level.

Poor quality engine oil or incorrect viscosity or type.
Oil is rated not only according to viscosity but also according to type. Some oils are not rated high enough for use in this engine. Check the specifications section in your manual and change to the correct oil.

Miscellaneous causes

Modification to exhaust system.
Most aftermarket exhaust systems cause the engine to run leaner, which makes them run hotter. When installing an accessory exhaust system, always reject the carburetors or tweak the fuel injection by means of an aftermarket black box. Invest in some dyno time to get the setup right.

Clutch problems

Clutch slipping

Clutch cable incorrectly adjusted.
Check and adjust.

Friction plates worn or warped.
Overhaul the clutch assembly.

Plain plates warped.

Clutch springs broken or weak.
Old or heat-damaged (from slipping clutch) springs should be replaced with new ones.

Clutch release mechanism defective.
Replace any defective parts.

Clutch centre or housing unevenly worn.
This causes improper engagement of the plates. Replace the damaged or worn parts.

Clutch not disengaging completely

Clutch cable incorrectly adjusted.
Check and adjust.

Clutch plates warped or damaged.
This will cause clutch drag, which in turn will cause the machine to creep. Overhaul the clutch assembly.

Clutch spring tension uneven.
Usually caused by a sagged or broken spring. Check and replace the springs as a set.

Engine oil deteriorated.
Old, thin, worn out oil will not provide proper lubrication for the plates, causing the clutch to drag. Replace the oil and filter.

Engine oil viscosity too high.
Using a heavier oil than recommended can cause the plates to stick together, putting a drag on the engine. Change to the correct weight oil.

Clutch release mechanism defective.

Loose clutch centre nut.
Causes housing and centre misalignment putting a drag on the engine. Engagement adjustment continually varies. Overhaul the clutch assembly.

Gear changing problems

Doesn't go into gear or lever doesn't return.

Clutch not disengaging.
See above.

Selector fork(s) bent or seized.
Often caused by dropping the machine or from lack of lubrication. Overhaul the transmission.

Gear(s) stuck on shaft.
Most often caused by a lack of lubrication or excessive wear in transmission bearings and bushings. Overhaul the transmission.

Selector drum binding.
Caused by lubrication failure or excessive wear. Replace the drum and bearings.

Gearchange lever return spring weak or broken.

Gearchange lever broken.
Splines stripped out of lever or shaft, caused by allowing the lever to get loose or from dropping the machine. Replace necessary parts.

Gearchange mechanism broken or worn.

Jumps out of gear

Selector fork(s) worn.
Overhaul the transmission.

Gear groove(s) worn.
Overhaul the transmission.

Gear dogs or dog slots worn or damaged.
The gears should be inspected and replaced. No attempt should be made to service worn parts.

Abnormal engine noise

Knocking or pinking

Carbon buildup in combustion chamber.
Use of a fuel additive that will dissolve the adhesive bonding the carbon particles to the piston crown and chamber is the easiest way to remove the buildup. Otherwise, the cylinder head will have to be removed and decarbonized. Rare with modern fuels.

Incorrect or poor quality fuel.
Old or improper fuel can cause detonation. This causes the pistons to rattle, thus the knocking or pinging sound. Drain the old fuel and always use the recommended grade.

Spark plug heat range incorrect.
Uncontrolled detonation indicates that the plug heat range is too hot. The plug in effect becomes a glow plug, raising cylinder temperatures. Install the proper heat range plug.

Improper fuel/air mixture.
This will cause the cylinders to run hot and lead to detonation. Clogged jets or an air leak can cause this imbalance.

Piston slap or rattling

Cylinder-to-piston clearance excessive.
Caused by improper assembly. Inspect and overhaul top-end parts.

Connecting rod bent.
Caused by over-revving, trying to start a badly flooded engine or from ingesting a foreign object into the combustion chamber. Replace the damaged parts.

Piston pin or piston pin bore worn or seized from wear or lack of lubrication.
Replace damaged parts.

Piston ring(s) worn, broken or sticking.
Overhaul the top-end.

Piston seizure damage.
Usually from lack of lubrication or overheating. Replace the pistons and have the cylinders rebored as necessary.

Connecting rod upper or lower end clearance excessive.
Caused by excessive wear or lack of lubrication. Replace worn parts.

Valve noise

Incorrect valve clearances.
Adjust the clearances.

Valve spring broken or weak.
Check and replace weak valve springs.

Camshaft or cylinder head worn or damaged.
Lack of lubrication at high rpm is usually the cause of damage. Insufficient oil or failure to change the oil at the recommended intervals are the chief causes.

Other noise

Cylinder head gasket leaking.

Exhaust pipe leaking at cylinder head connection.
Caused by improper fit of pipe(s) or loose exhaust flange. All exhaust fasteners should be tightened evenly and carefully. Failure to do this will lead to a leak.

Crankshaft runout excessive.
Caused by a bent crankshaft (from over-revving) or damage from an upper cylinder component failure. Can also be attributed to dropping the machine on either of the crankshaft ends.

Engine mounting bolts loose.
Tighten all engine mount bolts.

Crankshaft bearings worn.

Camshaft drive assembly defective.

Abnormal clutch noise

Clutch outer drum/friction plate clearance excessive.

Loose or damaged clutch pressure plate and/or bolts.

Transmission noise

Bearings worn.
Also includes the possibility that the shafts are worn. Overhaul the transmission.

Gears worn or chipped.

Metal chips jammed in gear teeth.
Probably pieces from a broken clutch, gear or shift mechanism that were picked up by the gears. This will cause early bearing failure.

Engine oil level too low.
Causes a howl from transmission. Also affects engine power and clutch operation.

Final drive noise

Chain not adjusted properly.

Front or rear sprocket loose.
Tighten fasteners.

Sprockets worn.
Renew sprockets.

Rear sprocket warped.
Renew sprockets.

Rubber dampers in rear wheel hub worn.
Check and renew.

Abnormal frame and suspension noise. Front end noise

Low fluid level or improper viscosity oil in forks.
This can sound like spurting and is usually accompanied by irregular fork action.

Spring weak or broken.
Makes a clicking or scraping sound. Fork oil, when drained, will have a lot of metal particles in it.

Steering head bearings loose or damaged.
Clicks when braking. Check and adjust or replace as necessary.

Fork yokes loose.
Make sure all clamp pinch bolts are tightened to the specified torque.

Fork tube bent.
Good possibility if machine has been dropped. Replace tube with a new one.

Front axle bolt or axle clamp bolts loose.
Tighten them to the specified torque.

Loose or worn wheel bearings.
Check and replace as needed.

Shock absorber noise

Fluid level incorrect.
Indicates a leak caused by defective seal. Shock will be covered with oil. Replace shock or seek advice on repair.

Defective shock absorber with internal damage.
This is in the body of the shock and can't be remedied. The shock must be replaced with a new one.

Bent or damaged shock body.
Replace the shock with a new one.

Loose or worn suspension linkage or swingarm components.
Check and replace as necessary.

Brake noise

Squeal caused by pad shim not installed or positioned correctly (where fitted).

Squeal caused by dust on brake pads.
Usually found in combination with glazed pads. Clean using brake cleaning solvent.

Contamination of brake pads.
Oil, brake fluid or dirt causing brake to chatter or squeal. Clean or replace pads.

Pads glazed. Caused by excessive heat from prolonged use or from contamination.
Do not use sandpaper, emery cloth, carborundum cloth, or any other abrasive to roughen the pad surfaces as abrasives will stay in the pad material and damage the disc. A very fine flat file can be used, but pad replacement is suggested as a cure.

Disc warped.
Can cause a chattering, clicking or intermittent squeal. Usually accompanied by a pulsating lever and uneven braking. Replace the disc.

Loose or worn wheel bearings.
Check and replace as required.

Oil pressure indicator light comes on

Engine lubrication system

Engine oil pump defective, blocked oil strainer gauze, or failed relief valve.
Carry out oil pressure check as per manual.

Engine oil level low.
Inspect for leak or other problem causing low oil level and add recommended oil.

Engine oil viscosity too low.
Very old, thin oil or an improper weight of oil used in the engine. Change to correct oil.

Camshaft or journals worn.
Excessive wear causing drop in oil pressure. Replace cam and/or cylinder head. Abnormal wear could be caused by oil starvation at high rpm from low oil level or improper weight or type of oil.

Crankshaft and/or bearings worn.
Same problems as above. Check and replace crankshaft and/or bearings.

Electrical system

Oil pressure switch defective.
Check the switch according to the procedure in your manual. Replace it if it is defective.

Oil pressure indicator light circuit defective.
Check for pinched, shorted, disconnected, or damaged wiring.

Excessive exhaust smoke

White smoke

Piston oil ring worn.
The ring may be broken or damaged, causing oil from the crankcase to be pulled past the piston into the combustion chamber. Replace the rings with new ones.

Cylinders worn, cracked, or scored.
Caused by overheating or oil starvation. The cylinders will have to be rebored and new pistons installed.

Valve oil seal damaged or worn.
Replace oil seals with new ones.

Valve guide worn.
Perform, or have performed, a complete valve job.

Engine oil level too high, which causes the oil to be forced past the rings.
Drain oil to the proper level.

Head gasket broken between oil return and cylinder.
Causes oil to be pulled into the combustion chamber. Replace the head gasket and check the head for warping.

Abnormal crankcase pressurization, which forces oil past the rings.
Clogged breather is usually the cause.

Black smoke
Carburettor models

Main jet too large or loose.
Compare the jet size to the Specifications in your manual.

Choke cable or linkage shaft stuck, causing fuel to be pulled through choke circuit.

Fuel level too high.
Check and adjust the float height(s) as necessary.

Float needle valve held off needle seat.
Clean the float chambers and fuel line and replace the needles and seats if necessary.

Black smoke
Fuel injection models

Fuel injection system malfunction.

Black smoke
All models

Air filter clogged.

Brown smoke
Carburettor models

Main jet too small or clogged.
Lean condition caused by wrong size main jet or by a restricted orifice. Clean float chambers and jets and compare jet size to specifications in your manual.

Fuel flow insufficient.
Float needle valve stuck closed due to chemical reaction with old fuel. Float height incorrect. Restricted fuel line. Clean line and float chamber and adjust floats if necessary.

Carburetor intake manifold clamps loose.

Faulty fuel pump.

Brown smoke
Fuel injection models

Fuel injection system malfunction.

Faulty fuel pump or pressure regulator.

Brown smoke
All models

Air filter poorly sealed or not installed.

Poor handling or stability

Handlebar hard to turn

Steering head bearing adjuster nut too tight.
Check adjustment as described in your manual.

Bearings damaged.
Roughness can be felt as the bars are turned from side-to-side. Replace bearings and races.

Races dented or worn.
Denting results from wear in only one position (e.g. straight ahead), from a collision or hitting a pothole or from dropping the machine. Replace races and bearings. Steering stem lubrication inadequate. Causes are grease getting hard from age or being washed out by high pressure car washes. Disassemble steering head and repack and/or replace bearings.

Steering stem bent.
Caused by a collision, hitting a pothole or by dropping the machine. Replace damaged part. Don't try to straighten the steering stem.

Front tire air pressure too low.

Handlebar shakes or vibrates excessively

Tires worn, out of balance or at incorrect pressures.

Swingarm bearings worn.
Replace worn bearings.

Wheel rim(s) warped or damaged.
Inspect wheels for runout.

Wheel bearings worn.
Worn front or rear wheel bearings can cause poor tracking. Worn front bearings will cause wobble.

Handlebar clamp bolts loose.

Fork yoke bolts loose.
Tighten them to the specified torque in your manual.

Engine mounting bolts loose.
Will cause excessive vibration with increased engine rpm.

Handlebar pulls to one side

Frame bent.
Definitely suspect this if the machine has been dropped. May or may not be accompanied by cracking near the bend. Replace the frame if it can't be safely straightened.

Wheels out of alignment.
Caused by improper location of spindle spacers or from bent steering stem or frame.

Swingarm bent or twisted.
Caused by age (metal fatigue) or impact damage. Replace the arm.

Steering stem bent.
Caused by impact damage or by dropping the motorcycle. Replace the steering stem.

Fork tube bent.
Disassemble the forks and replace the damaged parts.

Fork oil level uneven.
Check and add or drain as necessary.

Poor shock absorbing qualities

Too hard:
a) Fork oil level excessive.
b) Fork oil viscosity too high. Use a lighter oil (see the Specifications in your manual).
c) Fork tube bent. Causes a harsh, sticking feeling.
d) Shock shaft or body bent or damaged.
e) Fork internal damage.
f) Shock internal damage.
g) Tire pressure too high.
h) Suspension adjusters incorrectly set

Too soft:
a) Fork or shock oil insufficient and/or leaking.
b) Fork oil level too low.
c) Fork oil viscosity too light.
d) Fork springs weak or broken.
e) Shock internal damage or leakage.
f) Suspension adjusters incorrectly set

Braking problems

Brakes are spongy, or lack power

Air in brake line.
Caused by inattention to master cylinder fluid level or by leakage. Locate problem and bleed brakes. Cable problem on drum brakes.

Pad or disc (or drum/shoes) worn.

Brake fluid leak.

Contaminated pads/shoes.
Caused by contamination with oil, grease, brake fluid, etc. Clean or replace. Clean disc/drum thoroughly with brake cleaner.

Brake fluid deteriorated.
Fluid is old or contaminated. Drain system, replenish with new fluid and bleed the system.

Master cylinder internal parts worn or damaged causing fluid to bypass.

Master cylinder bore scratched by foreign material or broken spring.
Repair or replace master cylinder.

Disc warped/drum out of true.
Replace disc/drum.

Brake lever or pedal pulsates

Disc warped/drum out of true.
Replace/skim.

Spindle bent.
Replace spindle.

Brake caliper bolts loose.

Brake caliper sliders damaged or sticking (rear caliper), causing caliper to bind.
Lubricate the sliders or replace them if they are corroded or bent.

Wheel warped or otherwise damaged.

Wheel bearings damaged or worn.

Brakes drag

Master cylinder piston seized.
Caused by wear or damage to piston or cylinder bore. Incorrect cable/rod/shoe adjustment on drum systems.

Lever sticky or stuck.
Check pivot and lubricate.

Brake caliper binds on bracket (rear caliper).
Caused by inadequate lubrication or damage to caliper sliders.

Brake caliper piston seized in bore.
Caused by wear or ingestion of dirt past deteriorated seal.

Brake pad/shoe damaged.
Pad/shoe material separated from backing plate. Usually caused by faulty manufacturing process or from contact with chemicals. Replace.

Pads/shoes improperly installed.

Electrical problems

Battery dead or weak

Battery faulty.
Caused by sulphated plates that are shorted through sedimentation. Also, broken battery terminal making only occasional contact.

Battery cables making poor contact.

Load excessive.
Caused by addition of high wattage lights or other electrical accessories.

Ignition (main) switch defective.
Switch either grounds (earths) internally or fails to shut off system. Replace the switch.

Regulator/rectifier defective.

Alternator stator coil open or shorted.

Wiring faulty.
Wiring grounded (earthed) or connections loose in ignition, charging or lighting circuits.

Battery overcharged

Regulator/rectifier defective.
Overcharging is noticed when battery gets excessively warm.

Battery defective.
Replace battery with a new one.

Battery amperage too low, wrong type or size.
Install manufacturer's specified amp-hour battery to handle charging load.

Glossary

A

Accelerator pump A carburetor device for temporarily increasing the amount of fuel.

Air filter Either a paper, fabric, felt, foam, or gauze element through which the engine draws its air.

Air/fuel ratio Proportions in which air and fuel are mixed to form a combustible gas.

Alternator A generator of alternating current (a.c.) electricity.

ABS (Anti-lock braking system) A system that prevents the wheels from locking up under braking.

Ampere-hour (Ah) Measure of battery capacity.

Antifreeze A substance (usually ethylene glycol) mixed with water, and added to the cooling system, to prevent freezing of the coolant in winter.

Anti-dive System attached to the fork lower leg (slider) to prevent fork dive when braking hard.

Aspect ratio With a tire, the ratio of the section's depth to its width.

ATF Automatic Transmission Fluid. Often used in front forks.

Axle A shaft on which a wheel revolves. Also known as a spindle.

B

Backlash The amount of movement between meshed components. Usually applies to gear teeth.

Ball bearing A bearing consisting of a hardened inner and outer race with hardened steel balls between the two races.

BDC Bottom Dead Centre – denotes that the piston is at the lowest point of its stroke in the cylinder.

Bearings Used between two working surfaces to prevent wear of the components and a buildup of heat.

Belt drive Drive by a belt. Typical applications are for drive to the camshafts and transmission, and sometimes to the rear wheel.

Bevel gear Gear with slanted teeth, a pair of such gears turning the drive through ninety degrees.

BHP Brake horsepower.

Bias-belted tire Similar construction to radial tire, but with outer belt running at an angle to the wheel rim.

Big-end The larger end of a connecting rod and the one mounted on the crankpin.

Bleeding The process of removing air from an hydraulic system.

Bore Diameter of a cylinder.

Bore:stroke ratio The ratio of cylinder diameter to stroke. When these are equal the engine is said to be square.

Bottom Dead Centre (BDC) Lowest point of piston's stroke in the cylinder.

Bottom-end An engine's crankcase components and all components contained there-in.

BTDC Before Top Dead Centre in terms of piston position. Ignition timing is often expressed in terms of degrees or millimeters BTDC.

Bushing A cylindrical metal and/or rubber component used between two moving parts.

C

Caliper In a hydraulic brake system, the component spanning the disc and housing the pistons and brake pads.

Cam chain The chain that takes drive from the crankshaft to the camshaft(s).

Cam follower A component in contact with the camshaft lobes, transmitting motion to the valve gear.

Camshaft A rotary shaft for the operation of valve gear in poppet valve engines.

Carburetor Mixes variable volumes of air and fuel in the correct ratio.

Catalytic converter A device in the exhaust system of some machines that converts certain pollutants in the exhaust gases into less harmful substances.

Centrifugal To be thrown outwards. An outward force on an object moving around a point.

Charging system Description of the components that charge the battery.

Clutch A device for engaging or disengaging the engine from the driving wheel.

Coil spring A spiral of elastic steel.

Compression Squeezing smaller, particularly a fresh charge of mixture in the cylinder by the rising piston.

Compression damping Controls the speed the suspension compresses when hitting a bump.

Compression ratio The extent to which the contents of the cylinder are compressed by the rising piston.

Concentric Tending to a common center.

Connecting-rod The rod connecting the piston to the crankshaft via the big and small ends.

Constant rate A spring is this when each equal increment in load produces an equal change in length. (Contrast with multi-rate and progressive rate.)

Crankcase The chamber that carries the crankshaft.

Crankshaft A forged component, using the principle of the eccentric (crank) for converting the reciprocating piston engine's linear power pulse into rotary motion.

Cross-ply tire Form of tire construction in which the wraps of fabric in the tire carcass are laid over each other diagonally instead of radially (see radial ply).

Cush drive A shock-absorbing component in a transmission system.

Cylinder head Component closing the blind end of the cylinder. Houses the valve gear on a four-stroke engine.

D

Damper A device for controlling and perhaps eliminating unwanted movement in suspension systems.

Detonation Explosion of the mixture in the combustion chamber, instead of controlled burning. May cause a tinkling noise, known as pinking, under an open throttle.

Diaphragm The rubber membrane in a master cylinder or carburetor that seals the upper chamber.

Disc brake A brake design incorporating a rotating disc onto which the brake pads are squeezed.

Displacement The amount of volume displaced by the piston of an engine on rising from its lowest position to its highest.

Dog A projection from a moving part, mating with another dog or a slot. Used in gearboxes to connect two pinions on a shaft.

Double-overhead camshaft (DOHC) An engine that uses two overhead camshafts, one for the intake valves and one for the exhaust valves.

Downdraft Downward inclination of the induction tract, usually the carburetor too.

Dry sump Four-stroke lubrication system in which the oil is carried in a separate oil tank and not in the sump.

Duplex Two. A duplex frame has two front down tubes. A duplex chain has two rows of rollers (a simple chain has one).

E

Earth (ground) Usually the negative terminal of a battery, or part of the earth return.

Earth (ground) return The path of an electrical circuit that returns to the battery, utilizing the motorcycle's frame.

ECU (Electronic Control Unit) A computer that controls (for instance) an ignition system, or an anti-lock braking system.

EMS (Engine Management System) A computer controlled system that manages the fuel injection and the ignition systems.

Expansion chamber Section of two-stroke engine exhaust system so designed to improve engine efficiency and boost power.

F

Final drive Description of the drive from the transmission to the rear wheel. Usually by chain or shaft, but sometimes by belt.

Firing order The order in which the engine cylinders fire, or deliver their power strokes, beginning with the number one cylinder.

Flat twin (or four/six) An engine with horizontal adjacent or opposed cylinders, thereby having a flat configuration.

Float A buoyant object. Used in a carburetor to open and close the fuel inlet valve to maintain a constant fuel level.

Float chamber A carburetor component used to stabilize the fuel level in the carb.

Float level The height at which the float is positioned in the float chamber, so determining the fuel level.

Flywheel A rotating mass of considerable weight and radius, used to smooth out power impulses at the crank.

Four-stroke An operating cycle for an internal combustion engine in which combustion takes place on every other ascent of the piston. See also Two-stroke.

Free play The amount of travel before any action takes place, for example, the distance the rear brake pedal moves before the rear brake is actuated.

Friction The resistance between two bodies moving in contact with each other and relatively to each other.

Front fork Telescopic tubes incorporating springs and dampers used to provide a suspension system for the front of a motorcycle.

Fuel injection The fuel/air mixture is metered electronically and directed into the engine intake ports (indirect injection) or into the cylinders (direct injection). Sensors supply information on engine speed and conditions.

Fuel/air mixture The charge of fuel and air going into the engine.

Fuel level The level of fuel in a float chamber. Can be altered by changing the float level.

Fulcrum The point about which a leverage system pivots.

Fuse An electrical device that protects a circuit against accidental overload.

G

Gasket Any thin, soft material – usually cork, cardboard, asbestos or soft metal – installed between two metal surfaces to ensure a good seal.

Gear A component, often circular, with projections for the positive transmission of movement to a companion gear that may, or may not be, of the same shape and size.

Gearbox An assembly containing the transmission components used in varying the ratio of the gearing.

Gear ratio The ratio of turning speeds of any pair of gears or sprockets, derived from their number of teeth.

Ground Usually the negative terminal of a battery, or part of the earth return. See also: Earth/earth return.

H

Helical gears Gear teeth are slightly curved and produce less noise than straight-cut gears. Often used for primary drives.

HT High Tension Description of the electrical circuit from the secondary winding of the ignition coil to the spark plug.

HT lead A heavily insulated wire carrying the high tension current from the coil to the spark plug.

Horizontally-opposed A type of engine in which the cylinders are opposite to each other with the crankshaft in between.

Hub The centre part of a wheel.

Hydraulic A liquid-filled system used to transmit pressure from one component to another. Common uses on motorcycles are brake and clutch actuating mechanisms.

Hygroscopic Water absorbing. In motorcycle applications, braking efficiency will be reduced if DOT 3 or 4 hydraulic fluid absorbs water from the air – care must be taken to keep new brake fluid in tightly sealed containers.

Hypoid oil An extreme-pressure oil formulated to stand up to severe and unique conditions in hypoid transmission gears.

I

Ignition advance Means of increasing the timing of the spark at higher engine speeds. Done by mechanical means on early engines or electronically by the ignition control unit on later engines.

Ignition timing The moment at which the spark plug fires, expressed in the number of crankshaft degrees before the piston reaches the top of its stroke, or in the number of millimeters before the piston reaches the top of its stroke.

Injector Equipment for squirting a fluid. Used for both fuel and oil.

Inverted forks (upside down forks) The sliders or lower legs are held in the yokes and the fork tubes or stanchions are connected to the wheel axle (spindle). Less unsprung weight and stiffer construction than conventional forks.

J

Jet A hole through which air, fuel or oil passes, the size of the jet determining the quantity.

Joule The unit of electrical energy.

K

Kickstart A crank, operated by foot, for starting an engine.

Knock Similar to detonation, with same end results, but only the end gases in the far reaches of the combustion chamber ignite. The knocking sound, also known as pinging, occurs when the central and outer flame fronts meet.

L

Lambda (l) sensor A sensor fitted in the exhaust system to measure the exhaust gas oxygen content (excess air factor).

Land The raised portion between two grooves (e.g. between the ring grooves in a piston).

Layshaft In a "direct top gearbox" a gearbox shaft parallel to the mainshaft and carrying the laygears with which the mainshaft gears mesh to achieve ratio change.

lb-ft Pounds-force feet. An imperial unit of torque. Sometimes written as ft-lbs.

Leading link A form of front suspension using a pivoting link—approximately horizontal—with the axle in front of the pivot.

LT Low Tension Description of the electrical circuit from the power supply to the primary winding of the ignition coil.

Lubricant A substance, usually an oil, interposed between rubbing surfaces to decrease friction.

M

Main bearing The principal bearing(s) on which a component is carried but usually reserved exclusively for the crankshaft.

Mainshaft A principal shaft, as in an engine or a gearbox.

Master cylinder The operator end of an hydraulic control system.

Monoshock A single suspension unit linking the swingarm or suspension linkage to the frame.

Multigrade oil Having a wide viscosity range (e.g., 10W40). The viscosity ranges from SAE10 when cold to SAE50 when hot.

Multi-rate A spring that changes length unequally for equal increments of load. (Contrast with constant rate and progressive rate.)

N

Needle roller bearing A bearing made up of many small diameter rollers of hardened steel, usually kept separated by a cage. Often used where lubrication is poor.

Negative earth (ground) Using the negative or minus pole of the battery as the earth.

Nm Newton meters used to measure torque.

O

Odometer A mileage recorder.

Oil injection A system of two-stroke engine lubrication where oil is pump-fed to the engine in accordance with throttle position.

Oil pump A mechanically driven device for distributing oil around a four-stroke engine or pumping oil into a two-stroke engine.

Overhead valve (OHV) A four-stroke engine with the valves in the cylinder head and operated by pushrods.

Overhead cam (OHC) As above but with the camshaft contained in the cylinder head and operated by chain, gear or belt from the crankshaft.

P

Pinging The noise arising from Detonation and Knock.

Pitch The nominal distance between two specified points such as gear teeth, spring coils, or chain rollers.

Plug cap A cover over the top of a spark plug that transmits the HT voltage from the coil and lead to the plug.

Plug lead A heavily insulated wire carrying the high tension current from the coil to the spark plug.

Port Strictly, a hole or opening but also used to described the transfer ports in a two-stroke engine.

Power band The band of rpm in which the engine produces really useful power.

Pre-ignition Auto-ignition taking place before the desired moment and happening, not by sparking, but by incandescence.

Pre-load (suspension) The amount a spring is compressed when in the unloaded state. Pre-load can be adjusted by gas, spacer or mechanical adjuster. Determines ride height.

Premix The method of engine lubrication on older two-stroke engines. Engine oil is mixed with the petrol in the fuel tank in a specific ratio.

Primary gears The pair of gears connecting the crankshaft to the clutch in a unit construction engine.

Progressive rate A spring that progressively deflects less for equal increments in load (see Constant rate and Multi-rate).

Pushrod A stout rod used to transmit a push as in clutch or overhead-valve operation.

R

Radial ply tire Form of tire construction in which the wraps of fabric in the tire carcass are laid over each other radially, and not diagonally.

Radiator Device for losing heat.

Rake The angle of the steering axis from the vertical.

Rebore Removing the worn surface of a cylinder to create a new working surface.

Rebound damping A means of controlling the oscillation of a suspension unit spring after it has been compressed.

Rectifier Electrical device passing current in one direction only (and thus a wave), used to convert alternating current into direct current.

Reed valves A valve functioning like a reed, with pressure causing the "flap" to open or close.

Regulator Device for maintaining the charging voltage from the generator or alternator within a specified range.

Relay An electrical device used to switch heavy current on and off using a low current auxiliary circuit. Relays are used to switch heavy currents such as for the starter motor.

Rim The edge, margin or periphery. In the case of a wheel, the part that carries the tire.

Rising rate Condition set up using a three-way linkage between the swingarm and the shock absorber to give progressive suspension action.

Roller bearing One containing rollers as the support medium, and not balls.

rpm Revolutions per minute.

S

Seizure The binding together of two moving parts through pressure, temperature, or lack of lubrication, and often all three.

Shaft drive A method of transmitting drive from the transmission to the rear wheel.

Shock absorber A device for ironing out the effects of riding over bumps in the road to give a smooth ride.

Single-overhead camshaft (SOHC) An engine that uses one overhead camshaft to operate both intake valves and exhaust valves via rockers.

Small-end The smaller end on a connecting rod to which the piston is attached.

Spark plug Device for arcing an electric current, as a spark, between two electrodes inserted in the combustion space.

Spindle The fixed rod about which an article turns or perhaps swings in an arc (see Axle).

Sprocket Toothed wheel used in chain drive.

Stanchion In a telescopic front fork, that tubular part attached to the fork yokes and on or in which travels the moving slider.

Steering head The part of the frame that houses the steering stem.

Stroke The distance between the highest and lowest points of the piston's travel.

Subframe The rear part of a motorcycle frame that carries the seat, rear lighting and electrical components.

Sump Chamber on the bottom of a four-stroke engine that contains the oil.

Swingarm Supports the rear wheel and rear suspension.

T

Taper rollerbearing A hardened steel roller, being tapered instead of cylindrical.

Tachometer Rev-counter.

Thermostat Controls the flow of engine coolant into the radiator.

Timing The opening and closing points of valves and the moment of ignition in the engine cycle.

Top Dead Centre (TDC) Highest point of a piston's stroke.

Top-end A description of an engine's cylinder block, head and valve gear components.

Torque A twisting force about a shaft, measured in Nm, kgf m or lb ft.

Trail The distance between the point where a vertical line through the wheel axle touches the ground, and the point where a line through the steering axis touches the ground.

Twistgrip Rotary throttle control on the right handlebar, operated by twisting.

Two-stroke An operating cycle for an internal combustion engine in which combustion takes place on every ascent of the piston. The four events (induction, compression, ignition, exhaust) in the engine cycle are thus completed in two strokes (one up, one down) of the piston. See also Four-stroke.

U

Unsprung weight Anything not supported by the bike's suspension (i.e., the wheel, tires, brakes, final drive and bottom (moving) part of the suspension).

Upside-down forks (inverted forks) In contrast to conventional forks, these have the inner tube at the bottom, connected to the wheel axle, and acting as the slider, moving in the outer tube.

V

Valve A device through which the flow of liquid, gas, or vacuum may be stopped, started or regulated by a movable part that opens, shuts or partially obstructs one or more ports or passageways. The intake and exhaust valves in the cylinder head are of the poppet type.

Valve seat That part of the cylinder head against which the valve face seats and seals.

V-engine A motor with its cylinders arranged in V formation.

W

Watercooling Engine cooling system which uses a recirculating liquid coolant that passes through channels in the engine castings and externally through a radiator.

Water pump A mechanically driven device for moving coolant around the engine.

Wet sump Conventional four-stroke engine lubrication system in which the oil is carried in a pan (sump) on the bottom of the crankcase.

Wheelbase The distance between the axles of the front and rear wheels.

Y

Yokes Connect the steering stem to the front forks.

Index

Photos:
Tom Critchell,
John Noble,
Phillip Tooth,
Aprilia, BMW, CCM,
Ducati, Harley-Davidson,
Honda, Hyperbolt, Italjet,
Kawasaki, KTM,
Motorcycle Safety
Foundation, Suzuki,
Triumph, Yamaha

Author Acknowledgements:
Bob Gray
the late John Robinson,
Louise McIntyre,
Simon Larkin,
Luke Brackenbury,
Tom Critchell (again)
Lisa and Esme
Mark Brewin
Trevor Franklin
Garry Coull

Written by
Alan Seeley
Design
Simon Larkin
Technical editor
Martynn Randall
Editor
Peter McSean
Pat Hahn
Project Manager
Louise McIntyre